AND HE UNLEASHED ME TO THE WORLD

ROB RADOSTI

Published by Rob Radosti Ministries & Publications
237 N. Stephanie St. Suite E
Henderson, Nevada 89074 USA
www.RobRadosti.com

Printed for Worldwide Distribution in the United States of America.

THANKS AND DEDICATIONS

This book is dedicated to all who have been a part of my journey.

Thank you to my mother, Margaret, for loving me, pushing me forward and for praying for me, even in my darkest days. You always put me before yourself, and you taught me how to enjoy life. I love you.

Thank you to my father, Rob, for investing in me and loving me. I'm so thankful that our relationship was able to be reconciled. Your encouraging words in recent years have meant the world to me. I love you.

Thank you to the man who prophesied over me in my mother's womb in the early summer of 1984. I do not know your name, but we will meet one day.

Thank you to Robert Young for hugging me and receiving me while I was yet a practicing satanist. You gave me hope that real love truly existed.

Thank you to Rob Garret and Robert Young for investing hundreds of hours of mentoring into me. You helped launch me into my destiny.

Thank you to Darin and Carolina Torbert for standing with me in my call to the nations and for relentlessly serving those called to the mission field, often at the expense of your own well-being.

Thank you to my friend, Aaron Baltusis, for believing in me

and pointing me toward Jesus even when I had both feet over the flames of hell.

Thank you to Pastors Barry and Karen Fields for receiving me and Millie as your own children, supporting us, nurturing us, sending us, and saving our lives multiple times while on the mission field.

Thank you to Todd Bentley, who recognized God's call on me, mentored me in itinerant and evangelistic ministry and pushed me forward to make history.

Thank you to my dedicated editors, Kelly and Lisa. Without you, this book would not be a book. Your time was incredibly valued and appreciated.

Most of all, thank you to my beautiful wife, Millie Radosti. You fearlessly take on each day as if it is a special mission, all the while encouraging me onward in my call. You love and nurture our children, you serve others tirelessly and you have given up everything you have ever had time and time again for the call of the gospel. You are a true woman of God, and I'm so glad I married you. I love you.

To all the incredible men and women who have been a part of this journey, thank you. I look forward to spending eternity together. You have played a valuable role in the story of how **HE UNLEASHED ME TO THE WORLD.**

TABLE OF CONTENTS

Please be advised that this book contains some graphic content. Before you join me on my journey, I would like to clarify that when I speak of the kingdom of darkness, I do not do so to glorify it but to expose it. It is no coincidence that this book is in your hands right now, and my prayer is that you are both encouraged and wrecked by the presence of our Lord as you read this volume. May your heart be awakened as we journey together in making Jesus famous!

- **Rob**

TO OPEN THEIR EYES, *IN ORDER* TO TURN *THEM* FROM DARKNESS TO LIGHT, AND *FROM* THE POWER OF SATAN TO GOD, THAT THEY MAY RECEIVE FORGIVENESS OF SINS AND AN INHERITANCE AMONG THOSE WHO ARE SANCTIFIED BY FAITH IN ME.   ACTS 26:18

INTRODUCTION

Even before we walked through the doors, my wife and I sensed the thick darkness that awaited us. Although the organizers were Christians, everything was designed to bring in the lost from the streets. We found a small back room downstairs so that we could pray and then headed upstairs to discern the atmosphere of the event. As we worked our way through the darkness, we saw many young people dressed in Gothic attire who looked like they were auditioning for a part in the Adams Family. The crowd was packed with gang members and occultists, and we saw extreme body modification everywhere. The longer that we stayed at the concert, the faster our hearts beat until we retreated back to the small prayer room that we had found downstairs. We were fortunate enough to find two other people who were hungry to see God move, so we prayed again and asked God to pour out His Spirit in the club. The air was thick, the resistance was strong, and fear consistently attempted to assault us in our minds. During a break between band sets, the time finally came for me to give my testimony, and we made our way upstairs. We strategically positioned our team throughout the crowd so

1

Introduction

that they could pray with anyone in the audience who was receptive. I hesitantly made my way to the stage to take the microphone. I had never given my testimony in front of such a rough crowd before, and my imagination ran wild thinking of the grim possibilities that might lie ahead. The place was completely packed out with many young people who had driven from other states to see the featured band that was playing that night. The dark atmosphere added to my feeling of intimidation and just seemed to encourage those who glared at me... with Halloween makeup plastered all over their faces, of course.

I grabbed the microphone and stepped off the stage so that I was directly in front of the crowd. Silence fell throughout the club as I stood there trying to muster up the courage to say something. After introducing myself, I quickly dove into the details of my childhood and my journey into witchcraft and satan worship. Within just a few moments, some in the audience seemed to be drawn into what I was saying. As I spoke, a tall man with a harsh look on his face inched closer and closer to me. His face was painted with evil clown makeup, and he wore a hat with the symbol of a world-renowned gang. I glanced to the side of the stage to make sure Millie was okay, and I continued. "God is not a liar! Jesus revealed Himself to me!" I cried, as I related the details of how I had a powerful, life-changing encounter with Jesus Christ. "He delivered me from sin and bondage and gave me a new life, and He can do the same for you tonight! I know there is someone here who can identify with what I'm saying, and I want to talk to you tonight." I then challenged the crowd to pray and ask Jesus to reveal Himself to them. I also dared them to allow us to pray with them. Although the details are hazy, I can remember that I felt weak and shaky - until the name of

Jesus came out of my mouth. Suddenly, a great boldness fell on me, and I was able to finish speaking. I quickly moved in with Millie and our team to talk with people individually.

Within a few moments, my assistant whispered in my ear. "Rob, someone wants to see you outside... *alone.*"

"Oh boy," I thought. Sure enough, the man with the evil clown makeup who had been glaring at me menacingly wanted some privacy with me. I turned toward him, and he motioned in a most sinister fashion for me to follow him. As I trailed him down the stairs and out the door, all I could think was, "Lord, if it is my time, I guess I'll be seeing You any minute now." I then remembered seeing this same man in the middle of a switchblade fight with another gang member when we first arrived at the club. Uncertain about where we were going, I reluctantly followed him behind the building into a dark alley. He finally stopped and faced a brick wall. His back was turned to me, so I could not see his face. As I waited in suspense wondering what came next, he slowly turned, and revealed his tear-stained face with makeup smeared down his neck.

Between sobs, he managed to choke out, "How can I be saved; how can I know Jesus?!?" My thoughts quickly jumped from thinking I was going to get shot in a dark alley way to helping him respond to the Gospel right then and there!

"Kneel with me now!" I said in amazement. He dropped to the ground, took his hat off his head and threw it into the road. In tears, he relayed that he had recently been released from a mental hospital for murdering his younger

3

brother. Through his brokenness, he explained that years ago, he had a dream when voices spoke to him and told him to obey them by carrying out this evil deed. He confessed to all sorts of things that would make your flesh cringe, but in that moment, I knew that he needed to know the forgiveness of Jesus. I had been in this same situation - desperate to know that I could be forgiven. He was crying out from the pain and agony tormenting his heart. I looked him in the eyes, and I declared, "You are forgiven of these things because Jesus died for your sins and rose again, overcoming sin and death!" Without hesitating, he prayed with me and confessed Jesus as Lord.

As he prayed, he began to scream, "Fire! Fire! I feel fire in my chest!" He clutched at his chest as he fell to the ground. For a second, I wondered if I had prayed the wrong thing or if he was dying. Then Holy Spirit spoke to me and told me that He was bringing a fiery baptism to this young man from the inside out.

"This is the Holy Spirit!" I explained, "And you are a whole new person!" Suddenly, as we knelt there on the sidewalk, a car pulled up in front of us. Before I realized what was happening, the doors opened and out jumped two large men proudly sporting their loyalty to the opposing gang of my new-found friend. They began circling us as we knelt on the sidewalk in the dark.

"They're here to kill me!" the young man exclaimed.

"Well, at least we're going to heaven!" I exclaimed. We closed our eyes, prayed harder and braced for the worst. Suddenly, everything went quiet. We peeked out. No men. No car. No danger.

"We're alive!" the young man announced, lifting his face from the ground. I couldn't believe it! The men had just disappeared moments after threatening our lives. As we walked back toward the staircase, my new friend suddenly fell to the sidewalk, gripping his chest and rolling on the ground!

"What's going on!?" I shouted in disbelief.

"FIRE!" he shouted. "FIRE!" "My chest is on FIRE!" Peace washed over me as I understood that Holy Spirit was filling him with holy fire. "It was like fire in my chest that spread throughout my whole body!" he proclaimed as he rose from the sidewalk with tears in his eyes. I took him back inside where I hurriedly located a Bible to give him, and he hugged me and tearfully thanked me for sharing that night.

MY SO-CALLED CHILDHOOD

It was a muggy night in Hackettstown, New Jersey, during the summer of 1984, and little Maggie was just finishing up her shift at the local Shoprite. She pushed her red hair behind her ears and laid her hands gently on her baby bump. Just then, a man and his wife approached her checkout line.

"Excuse me, can we pray for your baby?" the friendly man asked. They explained that they were ministers of the gospel.

"Sure, I guess." said Maggie, somewhat taken aback. The preacher laid his hands on her belly and prayed that the child would be blessed and prosperous in the Kingdom of God and then prophesied that he would preach the Gospel with power.

Since I was the baby in little Maggie's womb, I can't quite remember what I was thinking at that moment. What I can tell you is that I don't know why, but I always had the strangest desire to be different. Throughout my childhood, I can remember that I always went to the extreme to be the different one, the one standing out in the crowd. I craved all of the attention yet also had my moments of bashfulness. I dreamed of foreign lands and what my life would be like in another nation. I had visions of both playing music and traveling, which were my two greatest desires. I have to admit, I'm not one for organization, so most of my crazy ideas were spur of the moment, "you've got to be kidding me" kinds of things. Only certain people were daring enough to embark on my very unique quests. Before I was drawn to the dark side, my innocence as a child was truly marked by a care-free, push-the-boundaries kind of attitude.

We had no television in the house, so I was always scaling the deepest edges of the woods near my home in Deltona, Florida, for something exciting. I was regularly sneaking out of the house at night roaming the streets, looking at the stars and pondering what someone on the other side of the globe was doing at that moment. I also always wondered where my true love was and what she was doing at that moment. I was truly open to the possibilities and wonders of what awaited me on the other side of my own little world.

Shortly after our move to Florida in 1986, my parents began to attend a local Seventh-Day Adventist Church. My mom had been raised in the SDA community, and she had introduced my dad to it after I was born. Together, my parents quickly became adherents to its teachings and beliefs, and my world as a young boy began to change. I was put into a church school in the denomination that had mandatory uniforms that I just could not stand. I was also raised a vegetarian due to the religious convictions of my parents. Every week from Friday night sundown to Saturday night sundown, we kept the Sabbath. We were not to participate in any kind of labor whatsoever. We did not own a television and were not permitted to spend money or exert energy that would be considered working.

I was never allowed to go to the movies, nor was I allowed to congregate where worldly people did or associate myself with "sheep of different folds" on any day of the week. I remember many Sabbaths playing outside, carefully trying to determine in my heart if what I wanted to do would be too much work, thus breaking the Sabbath. For example, I loved to build tree houses, ride my bike and play with my toys, but I was never quite sure where to draw the line. If the family desired to do something on the Sabbath, it was ultimately up to Dad to decide whether it would take too much effort to be done on that day.

Dancing and any style of music that involved drums or a beat were off limits any day of the week. The SDA church began when a woman who lived in the late 1800s named Ellen G. White began to have supernatural encounters. She wrote down her visions, and the visitors in her visions outlined for her the true way that things were to be done, such as keeping the Jewish Sabbath, abstaining from unclean meats and not adorning oneself with jewelry or makeup. Eventually, her writings became heralded as equal to the Bible itself, and she became known as *"the spirit of prophecy."* Every Friday and Saturday night, my family and I would attend "Vespers." Vespers is a word which is derived from the Medieval Latin word *vesperae* and means "evening star." The services both ushered in and closed out the Sabbath, and I always looked forward to them. To me, it was more of a sign of freedom than anything else, and as soon as it was over each week, we went out to get frozen yogurt and went mini-golfing together as a family.

As a child I loved to have fun, but certain things that were not exciting for me did pose a challenge. As for my learning habits, I just couldn't seem to do well in school. I was constantly caught day dreaming instead of learning. I also lived to play practical jokes on my teachers. At the young age of nine, I started to act like a troublemaker on the school grounds. One day during reading class, I grew very bored, and I watched anxiously as my teacher, Ms. Meyers, strolled down the hall to the bathroom. She was a very nice lady, but she had glasses as big as tennis balls and didn't seem to be getting married anytime soon. She used to do a funny sort of sideways thing with her lips, which made me picture a blue bonnet of some sort on her head.

As soon as she disappeared out of sight, I ran to my backpack and tore it open to find my favorite tape with a copy of the song "Sweat (Everybody Dance Now)." I had secretly turned on the radio behind my mom and dad's back a few days before and recorded the song onto a cassette. I eagerly shoved it into the tape player that was used for science class in the back of the classroom and jumped on the desk and started to wiggle my hips and pull my zipper down as I grooved to the music. The classroom filled with the beloved disco-dance song, and the students sat with their jaws dropped open, both shocked and horrified. All the students at the school knew that kind of music was off limits, and they probably couldn't believe I was shaking my booty in front of everyone.

9

My So-Called Childhood

The teacher came back just in time to hear the end of the song from down the hall and glimpsed me scurrying away and hiding in a cubbyhole. That afternoon, my mother was called in for a parent-teacher conference concerning the unacceptable and disgusting display of her son's behavior. I was grounded for a while and almost suspended. As awful as it was, I was always interested in pushing the limits because it seemed like there was no one else on the face of the earth who wanted to see something *exciting* happen.

I thrived on attention, so for a time, I resorted to chasing girls all over the school, pinning them down and kissing them. I had quite the reputation for a little scrawny white boy in a religious school. On one occasion, my friends and I snuck down the hall while our teachers were out of the room and threw paper airplanes into the other classrooms via the windows conveniently located above our lockers. Usually, Mr. Fisher's bald head was our target, and most of the time, our aim was exact. My friends and I regularly got on the desks and danced with our shirts off and our pants down. We simply terrorized the class.

While I was in my second year of seventh grade, we even threw a ball around the room and accidentally hit the clock, which loosened it from the wall. I heard my teacher coming, so we scurried back to our places and sat down in feigned innocence. To my surprise, when Mr. Anderson returned, he pulled his desk into the middle of the classroom for the next social studies lesson - right below the clock! A few seconds into the lesson, we heard a few warning creaks and... CRASH! The clock dropped right on his head and shattered into pieces. It was the funniest thing the class had ever seen, and I got lots of props for it.

And He Unleashed Me to the World   **Rob Radosti**

My friend Scott and I instigated many of the incidents at school. Scott wore glasses as big as melons and was the kind of kid who laughed at any funny sound you made during class. One day, we were sitting in the hallway when a lovely little bee landed on the window, which was about five feet high and a few feet long. He was allergic to bees, so he looked for something to use to kill it. However, the closest thing he could find was a tennis racket. Before I could utter a word, the entire whopping five feet of glass shattered all over our heads. As I pulled pieces of glass out of my skin and his neck, he sat there cracking up at what he had just done. He thought it was funny until he had to do chores for a month to buy the school a new window.

My fellow classmates waited on the edge of their seats watching to see what kind of daredevil trick or fearless feat I would attempt next. On the more serious side, it seemed purely coincidental that I often came so close to destruction. As I grew older, I knew that it was more than just a coincidence. An invisible enemy seemed to frequently attempt to destroy me throughout my childhood.

While some labeled me as paranoid, I am not talking about the times that I broke bones or even the time that I fell out of a 45-foot tree. I remember one instance when I was about seven years old and at the park with my parents. I paced anxiously back and forth in front of the bathroom for a few minutes as I tried to decide if I should go in alone or not. My parents had taught me not to leave their side, yet my Dad often teased me by hiding. For instance, one year at Sea World, he disappeared for a whole five minutes. To a young boy, the time seemed like an eternity. Unbeknownst to me, he was watching me the whole time as I cried and screamed, "I'm lost!" He thought it was hilarious.

11

My So-Called Childhood

As I paced in front of the bathroom, I had a strange feeling about going in alone. The problem with me was that I usually ignored my better judgment just for the thrill of it all. Just as I was about to open the door, some police officers rushed past me into the bathroom. I watched in disbelief as my parents hurried to my side. Within a minute the policemen exited with a wanted kidnapper who was hiding behind the door.

I can also remember in fourth grade, the year we started that horrible division in math class. I was quietly taking a test along with my classmates one morning in Mr. Feist's class. Suddenly, I heard and felt a low rumbling throughout the building that softly shook my desk. It felt like an earthquake. I tried to recall if earthquakes happened regularly in Florida. I knew that I had never felt one before if that is what it was. I looked up to see the principal watching his desk shake as well. He and I were the only ones who seemed to notice it, and we looked up from our work as our eyes locked. We silently communicated, "Did you feel that too?" Everyone else was busily taking their tests. I felt strange inside, a morbid kind of feeling, as if the spirit of death had just entered the room.

Just then, Mr. Feist left to go to the bathroom, so I reluctantly continued taking my test. After a little while, I had to use the bathroom, too. As I made my way to the facilities, I didn't realize that the principal had been gone for a half hour. I walked directly to the middle stall because for some reason, I had a weird phobia about the end stalls. As I opened the door, a putrid odor rose from the tiles at my feet. I looked down and screamed in sheer horror at the sight. The principal was curled up like a pretzel, half on the toilet and half on the floor. His eyes were wide open, and he was as white as a ghost. His shattered glasses had broken all over the floor, and bile and vomit mixed with other bodily fluids on the ground.

I was so frightened that I ran to the nearest classroom and screamed, "The principal is dead in the bathroom!" I watched in horrified disappointment as everyone in the room started to laugh at me. Because of my reputation, they assumed it was a joke or prank. I suppose I deserved it for "crying wolf" so many times.

Within minutes, the ambulances arrived, and he was pronounced dead on the scene from a heart attack. It was the first time that I had come face to face with death, and it seemed that from that day forward, death began to follow me. Thoughts of Mr. Feist would haunt me for years to come, even to the point where I cut him out of every picture in my school yearbooks so that I would not have nightmares.

Shortly thereafter, my grandmother with whom I was very close passed away from lung cancer due to smoking her whole life. Within weeks, one of my new best friends, age 10, died of cystic fibrosis.

Just before Grandmother Marie passed away, I remember that she asked me to make a promise to her. She had just accepted Christ and been baptized in the Seventh Day Adventist church, and she asked me to promise never to dabble in witchcraft or sorcery. I loved fantasy stories and frequently pretended to have magical powers. I made the promise anyway since I loved her so much, and I remembered our words as I stood over her casket. At the time, it was not difficult to make such a promise because we did not own a television. Years later, I would understand the important role that the vow would mean to my future. Unfortunately, I slowly began to break that promise.

The Day a Part of Me Died

When my mom and I were on vacation a few years later in New Jersey, my dad called to privately speak to my mom. He was my hero, so the possibility of anything bad happening never crossed my mind. After hours of hiding in a closet, my mother emerged an emotional wreck like nothing I had ever seen before. After 14 years of marriage, my parents were splitting up. I was never given many details, but I was told that he had given up his position as a lay pastor at our local SDA church. He had found another woman and was pursuing a career in law enforcement. I recall many arguments over his desire to work in law enforcement because of the effect and stress it would have on our family. My mother was a loving woman when I was young but did suffer from her own childhood trauma along with other issues. She had a fiery temper known by everyone and had the red hair to match. I cannot deny that she had a serious problem with angry outbursts, and my father just could not take it anymore. We had a few typical problems, but up until this point, I thought we were one of the closest families on the planet.

The morning that I woke up and saw that my dad was really gone was the day that a part of me died. I was in counseling for a while, and they told me that I was exhibiting signs of being bi-polar and having chronic depression. One day at the tender age of 12, I stood facing the mirror feeling intense self-hatred. "You are the reason your dad left," I muttered to my reflection. As I looked into my own eyes, many questions came to mind, such as "What are you? Why are you here? Would anyone even care if you weren't?" No one had to tell me how to commit suicide; it was like I woke up one morning and just knew what to do. I held a knife to my wrist as I stared into my reflection yet again. My life flashed before my eyes, and the realization that I would never see my mom or friends again hit me hard. If I followed through, I would not see my new brother grow up, and most of all, I had no idea what would happen after I died. I again found myself wondering if I was the only one who ever thought about what was beyond my four walls. A strange fascination with death began to form within me.

We had been praying for a sibling for me for a very long time, and it seemed that God had finally heard and granted our request just before the split. Although it was a joy to meet my new baby brother as I again and again overcame the powerful urge to take my own life, we were all devastated by the divorce. It quickly became clear that both my mom and I had lost any of the religious faith that we had left. We soon became very bitter toward God. I did not want to even think about this loving "Jesus" that I had been taught about. He didn't seem to be able to heal any of the sick people that I knew or help any of us. Why should I care anymore? I watched my mom begin going out to bars at night and coming home very late. Soon, a friend of hers moved into our house to help with the living expenses. Within a few days, I was left alone with this woman. As soon as my mom left, her housemate told me that we were going to the beach. I was very excited because I loved to swim, and I loved the outdoors. We left in her car and arrived at the beach about a half hour later. As I exited the car, I knew instantly that I did not recognize this beach. We walked toward the sand, and I saw women and men walking around, basking in the sun and swimming – in the nude! I had never heard of a nude beach, and I knew my mom wouldn't want me to be at one. The woman left me alone and went down the beach a ways, and I watched her remove her bathing suit and lie down in the sun. As I walked around in shock, I could not help but feel unsafe and alone. This reminded me of the helpless feeling I had when I was taken advantage of by a 14-year-old girl who lived down the street from me. However, I never told anyone. Just a few days later, my mom kicked her roommate out of our house after finding drugs hidden in the dresser drawers of her room.

Each of these incidents birthed a greater desire in me to experience what the world had to offer. One day, I began to beg my Mom to put me in public school. I felt that if I could experience public school, I could finally find the identity that I was looking for and be accepted by the world. I always seemed to be the odd man out, the one who had to be taught all of the naughty terms that my neighbors used and the one that did not get the dirty jokes. That year, I was enrolled in the seventh grade at Galaxy Middle School in Deltona, Florida. The transition from a sheltered childhood and a class of nine kids to a school with seemingly thousands of worldly wise and spoiled students was a death wish for me.

AWAKENING TO DARKNESS

rejection

I had only been attending public school for a couple of weeks, and not only did I not find acceptance, but I found the opposite. I was butchered everyday by the popular people with name-calling, threatening and beating. A root of racism was planted in my heart due to the Hispanic gangs that constantly threatened my life during this time. I spent my nights in shock, wondering if the next day at school would be my last. I drained slowly from the sink of life, growing more and more depressed by the day. The most popular lifestyle scene when I went to middle school was that of a *skater*. I tried to mimic what I saw in style and attitude, but I was continually labeled a "poser" no matter how I dressed or what kind of skateboard I had. I became determined to fit in and have friends. One day, I stumbled across a boy named Aaron. He was raised as a Christian, and because he was a goofball, he reminded me of friends that I had in the past. I started to hang out with him here and there, and we began to develop a strong friendship.

17

Awakening to Darkness

Even though I had found one friend, I still had a growing darkness inside of me that Aaron noticed. As I observed the styles of the other kids at school, I finally could identify with something. One day as I walked down the hall to my next class, I noticed that the boy walking toward me looked unlike anyone I had ever seen before. He was ugly. **Very** ugly. In fact, he was clearly ugly by choice - he actually looked dead! As he approached me, I stopped to talk to this walking corpse. He had black nails and dark circles around his eyes that resembled a raccoon. He wore a long black trench coat that nearly covered his black platform combat boots.

"Excuse me, what are you?" I asked as I observed the ripped up fishnet stockings on his arms.

"We're the freaks," he replied.

"What's that?" I asked, now more interested.

"We're the dark ones that everyone makes fun of," he related.

"Everyone makes fun of them?" I thought to myself. My mouth opened and out came "Hey, I'm a freak too! Everyone makes fun of me and wants to beat me up! I don't fit in anywhere, and I love dark things! Would you mind if I hung out with you?"

"Sure, let's hang out!" he answered to my surprise. "I'm Vince," he introduced himself.

"Rob!" I responded. As we walked, I suddenly began to feel important and wanted to do whatever was necessary to join this group of... well, what looked like vampires to me.

"So what kind of music do you listen to?" asked Vince. Now that was a tricky question. Since I was taught that most music besides the Maranatha Singers, Keith Green and Psalty the Singing Songbook was of the devil, I wasn't sure what to say. I had never really listened to music with a beat or with drums in it since it was off limits.

"Oh, just whatever's on the radio, I guess...." I replied, grinning nervously.

"Well, I've got some great cassettes here if you'd like to borrow them; you'll love them!" exclaimed Vince.

"Oh sure, wow, thanks!" I responded, trying to hide my excitement. I took one or two of the tapes that he offered me, and we exchanged contact information and went to our next classes. I could hardly contain my emotions as I boarded the bus home later that day knowing that my Mom would still be at work when I arrived. I would have free reign of her stereo system that she kept in her room. She was not going to be home until late, so I moved it to my room overnight. As I popped in one of the tapes later that evening, the sound that assaulted my ears from the speakers was certainly something I had never heard before, nor was I even able to classify it as music at the moment. In my opinion, it resembled a case of rather bad gas, so I took out the cassette booklet in an attempt to read the lyrics as I could not understand a word.

Screams, growls and drums that sounded like machine guns blasted from the sound system, and before long, I had grown very fond of the music. I began to feel a

19

Music

courage, a boldness that I had not felt before. Then I read the lyrics – and I found out why. Never in my wildest imagination had I ever thought of writing a song for the sole purpose of destroying Christianity and blaspheming the name of Jesus! Now I was listening to just such a song. As I listened, the message sank deeper and deeper into my soul.

I played the music all night long and woke up the next day feeling very empowered. I went to school and told my friend Vince how incredible my night was and how much I loved the music and identified with it.

"Want some more?" he asked.

"Sure!" I answered. Within a couple of days, I felt that I had finally discovered who I was... well, almost. The following Monday morning, I returned to school and met up with Vince, who I now considered my best friend. My Christian friend, Aaron, began to take notice of who I was hanging out with and warned me and told me that he was praying for me. I ignored him.

Identity

"So like, how do I really become one of you?" I questioned Vince. I noticed that he walked around with a medium-sized group who all looked like something out of the Rocky Horror Picture show.

"You really want to be one of us?" he asked.

"Yes!" I replied intently. He then reached into his backpack and pulled out a black book.

"Take this home, and study it. Do what it says. You

will love it, and you will be one of us." said Vince.

"Thanks man!" I shouted as I grabbed the book and tossed it in my book bag. That afternoon when I arrived home, I was determined to find out if the book could give me as much power as Vince claimed. I grabbed it out of my bag and read the name to myself. It was "The Satanic Bible" by Anton Szandor LaVey. I was amazed. All I ever knew before was the boring Bible, which had a bunch of rules and regulations and a couple of seemingly inspirational fables about some guy who manifested fish and healed diseases. THIS however, this was an amazing discovery for me. Why? Because for some time, I had felt that perhaps the dark side could offer me more identity, more truth and more power than reading a memory verse at night ever could. I cracked it open.

As I began to read the Satanic Bible, I felt an overwhelming sense of power come to me, one that no other religion or practice could ever offer. Just to be sure, I grabbed my "Psalty the Singing Songbook Kid's Bible" that my parents had gotten me as a gift when I was a wee lad, and I opened the pages as well. Before long, I was comparing them to each other and demanding that both sources of power, if real, reveal themselves at once to show me where the true power was. Within just a few moments of reading the Holy Bible, I knew it was not what I was looking for or so I thought at the moment.

That day, I began to speak to satan and told him that if he was real, I would sell him my soul if he would give me what I wanted. You might wonder what that was. I wanted to destroy God and Christianity, and I wanted power - power to make people do anything I wanted. I wanted power to

21

turn people from the God of the Christians by proving to them that He was a liar. I wanted power to cause all those who had harmed me or threatened me to suffer. I went to school the next day and told Vince about the encounter that I had the night before. He seemed happy and introduced me to the rest of the gang. I was now a satanist, and I was proud of it. I went on to build a satanic altar in my closet where my mom never looked. I burned candles and kept satanic music playing in the walk-in closet 24/7.

Due to my growing desire to be like the rest of the satanic group, I started dabbling in my mom's makeup drawer when she left for work. I didn't have a way to get to a mall, and I had no money, so I decided that this was the best way to begin to express who I was with my looks. I had struggled with gender identity from a young age and was happy to finally be able to experiment with makeup. I remember the day that I strolled down the hallway at school, sporting my mom's red lipstick, yellow eye shadow and pantyhose. I was threatened cruelly throughout the day, and one of my good friends promised to get me some darker makeup and teach me how to look gothic. After school, I went over his house. He painted my face and eyes with dark make-up and gave me some black nail polish. I began to wear T-shirts that promoted a certain rock star who was a voice in my movement. I found myself strangely drawn to this man. Within just a month or two in public school, I had dyed my hair black and decided to grow it out. Of course, I also began to shave it underneath in the style of the early '90s.

The music I was listening to helped me express the hatred and darkness that I felt inside for life and for what had happened to my family. I began to wear ripped

22

stockings on my arms and to paint my nails black. Sometimes I would go as far as cross-dressing, no matter what kind of criticism it cost me. I even began to question my sexuality. I wanted pleasure, pain, power and most importantly, anything that would keep me at polar opposites with God.

A few days after my dramatic "conversion," I sat in class with "war paint" make-up on my face and my nails painted black, staring at band pictures that I had hidden in my binder. I was only 12 years old! I felt so alone and was continuing to fight frequent thoughts of suicide.

As I looked to my right, I noticed a funny-looking kid with gigantic glasses staring at a video-game magazine. "That's stupid," I thought. As I continued to watch him, I realized that he had the same kind of passion for those video games that I had for my style and music. I also noticed that he had no friends, similar to me who only had a few. I was bored out of my mind, so I struck up a conversation with him. We decided to hang out that evening so that he could introduce me to some video games. What surprised me was that he did not judge me by the way that I looked even with eyeliner on my eyes!

Mike and I quickly became close friends apart from my best friend, Vincent, and we accepted each other the way that we were. We became like brothers, and I slept at his house often. One night, when I was sleeping over, I learned that his older brother had just been released from prison that day. That night while I slept on the floor in Mike's room, his older brother barged in and dragged me into his room while I was half-asleep and scared to death.

23

Awakening to Darkness

My vision was blurred, and as I focused, I saw a group of what looked like college-aged low-lifes partying, drinking beer and touching each other sexually. As I came to, everyone stopped and stared at me. One of the men took a bag of white powder out of his shirt and offered me some. Another man handed me what looked like a small, fat cigarette and told me to inhale it as deeply as I could. I was confused and scared that they were going to hurt me, so I tried the things they offered me. I did not know what I was doing, but I did not want to tick them off, so I agreed to do as they said. I was handed a small glass with what looked like water but smelled horrendous and was told to drink it. Reluctantly, I did and then begged them to let me go back to sleep. They continued to make me drink, and before long, I became dizzy and nearly passed out. As I was in and out of consciousness, they began to make me touch them inappropriately. I was scared, tired and felt horribly violated.

Eventually, I woke up on the floor in Mike's room the next morning, but no one would believe me when I told them what happened. After that experience, I felt so dirty and violated that I craved whatever substances they gave me that night just to escape from the memories. I started to smoke cigarettes with friends around the neighborhood, and Mike and I began to steal his parent's alcohol from their cabinets and get drunk. Mike became heavily involved in the drug scene due to his brother's influence. His style of clothing contrasted starkly with mine. His style of music also greatly differed from mine; he now loved listening to the Backstreet Boys. Although I kept my gothic trend, our friendship never wavered. I became so messed up that I ended up failing the seventh grade that year.

The next year, I turned 13, and my mom, my brother,

Ryan, and I moved back to a small town in New Jersey near where I was born. My mom's new boyfriend trailed behind us, and they were married shortly thereafter. My mother was attempting to reestablish her faith and teach my new stepfather about it as well. I wanted nothing to do with it, and frankly, neither did he. I found that out for sure one day when I was home alone. I was messing around with his new computer and found a box hidden away on a shelf containing three hardcore pornographic videos. I watched them, immediately became addicted and called all of my friends over for movie parties when I was home alone.

After unsuccessfully trying another year of public school, I was again stuck in a different private Seventh-Day Adventist school, this time in another state. Now, I was the new and experienced kid on the block. I felt worth a million bucks! I began to wear my anger and depression on my sleeve, especially in encounters with a teacher that I hated. We would get into frequent arguments, and it was not uncommon for him to raise his fist to my face. I proceeded to throw rocks through his windshield and to declare bomb threats on the school. I was suspended and nearly put in juvenile detention.

I had grown a deep-rooted hatred and rebellion towards Christians. At the time, I only knew of Seventh-Day Adventists because we were not allowed to communicate with so-called "Sunday worshippers." Any time I showed up at church with dyed hair or an earring, the members judged me and told my mom that she was not raising me correctly. This really upset me.

By the time I finally moved to the ninth grade and into a private academy, I again found myself communicating

25

with the powers of darkness. I cursed the teachers and deliberately wore things to school that were not allowed so that I would get sent home. Once, I attempted to walk the nearly five miles to my home, but fortunately, a friend picked me up along the way. I was literally praying curses over those people and hoping that they would die. I took a French class because linguistics and culture was one of the very few subjects that held my interest as far as school was concerned.

When I wasn't stuck in academy, some of my next-door neighbors and I went to the local skating rink in Hackettstown where we called ourselves the gods of the roller rink. We would show off our superior skating skills, meet girls and get into trouble. Around this time, I met a nice girl who was a little older than me, and we started a relationship. She held tightly to the Seventh-Day doctrine and morals although before long she couldn't help but bend them for me. We were very opposite, yet the relationship lasted for nine months. I believed that I was going to marry her. She did not like my music, and since I was trying to form a Goth band at the time, I knew it would not work between us. I cut the relationship off and continued hosting a world of drugs, heavy alcohol, pornography, fantasy and witchcraft right in my own bedroom. Some nights, I sat outside a local liquor store until 4 a.m. waving a $20 bill as I begged for someone to buy me some booze.

One day, I began to have visions of the spirit world, and they continued through the night. The house we lived in was a former funeral home from the 1800s, and that made it all the better for me. One night, a large gray orb or spherical body awoke me. I followed it down the stairs and into my parent's room where it disappeared. As I cried out to the spirits for more power, things began to move during the night. For example, I leaned my guitar against my bed, and the next morning, it would be on the other side of the room after my door had been locked all night. One night, I woke up to my bed shaking violently and levitating as I listened to a satanic song on my Disc-man.

I finally decided that I was done for good with private school and that after the summer I would take the bus to the public high school in Hackettstown. I sought friends in the area, and I believed I would find them there. Every summer, I flew to Florida to visit my dad for a month or two, but the majority of my time was spent with my friends from middle school, mainly Aaron and Mike. My dad was a different person, and I was not sure how to relate to him anymore.

Even so, I liked going to Florida. Not only was it my homeland, but I could do almost anything I wanted with no religious restriction at all at my dad's house. The only exception was when I was around Aaron, my Christian friend. Although he respected me, he grew more concerned as I dove deeper into spiritual darkness. Another reason that I liked Florida was because I could visit one of the largest spiritist hubs in the nation, Cassadaga. The Cassadaga Cemetery had what was called "the devil's chair." Supposedly, you could speak with satan and sell him your soul all over again if you sat on it on Halloween night. I liked that idea.

While in Florida during the summer of 1999, I introduced my friend, Mike, to the Ouija board. I was already building my own, and he loved the idea. Together, we started practicing talking to spirits and demons through

27

the Ouija boards that we obtained or made. I gradually found myself relying more and more on these boards for guidance in my personal life. I would ask them what was going to happen in the future and what I should do about certain situations. The answers were usually right, but not 100 percent of the time.

One night, a specific demon refused to leave the house and would not let us sleep. We closed the Ouija board and threw it into the closet. "That's enough!" we exclaimed. Suddenly, we heard loud crashing noises in the kitchen and ran out to see what was happening. Every kitchen cabinet was opening and glasses, plates, cups and bowls were flying out all at once, shattering all over the floor. The back door of the house then began to slam violently by itself.

At about 3 a.m., I finally decided to head back to my dad's house. I carefully opened the door to my half-brother's room where I was sleeping. I was exhausted and a bit spooked because I felt like something had followed me home. As soon as I shut the door behind me, I turned to see little Eric standing straight up in his crib. He began screaming loudly, yet his eyes remained shut as if he were asleep. His crib was shaking violently, so I slammed the door and decided to sleep on the couch in the living room instead. I figured that the demon would follow me and leave my little brother in peace. As soon as I lay down on the couch, the TV suddenly switched on. I reached for the remote and powered it off. About an hour later, I awoke to the sound of the oven fan turning on. I got up and switched it off. "Did anyone come out here at 4 a.m. and turn on the oven fan?" I asked the next morning. Everyone denied getting up and turning on either the fan or the TV. Things were starting to spiral out of control.

Back in New Jersey the following school year, I reluctantly stepped into tenth grade. I found many more young people there into the dark scene than in my school in Florida years earlier, and I got to know some of them very quickly. Under their influence, I now sported a black trench coat with some form of weapon underneath, usually chains, a satanic bible, and the ability to manipulate things with my mind without a Ouija board. Our little cult was not very well-liked by the other groups, especially the Hispanics. We had regular run-ins with them, which often resulted in life or death circumstances. One day, they showed up at my job at K-Mart and slashed our group's tires. Within a few days, it was our turn to laugh as we watched their leader get busted for paraphernalia, possession, and drug trafficking. We were a miserable little Goth family, performing séances together in the graveyard, studying the satanic bible together and comparing our sword and weaponry collections.

Our leader was eventually expelled from school for making bomb threats, and that required me to step it up a notch. I was 16 years old and started a relationship with a witch that I met at school. I moved in with her for a time, and she began to teach me everything she knew about witchcraft. Her favorite book was a handbook for witches. I began to learn how to cast spells, commune with the dead, read palms, and often subjected myself to voluntary demonic possession. There was a person who had been involved with my girlfriend prior to our relationship who I vowed to kill. He was from the country of Chile and had just returned home. I didn't care if I had to fly there someday to do it. This just confirmed my hatred for Hispanic people.

29

Awakening to Darkness

Whenever we had a coven in my girlfriend's basement, unbelievers would come and would leave converted to satanism and witchcraft. I hated school with a passion and called my mother and threatened to drop out. I argued that if she did not sign papers and give me permission, I would do it anyway, and they would come and arrest her. Needless to say, I dropped out of school at the beginning of my tenth grade year. I was a suicidal alcoholic who drank straight vodka from morning to evening. I dove deeper into satan worship, smoked drugs frequently, considered myself to be a warlock and accepted the fact that I was chronically depressed. I cannot even explain to you the things that I saw and did, nor should I in this book. The purpose for telling as much as I already have is to prepare the way for the coming of the King in my life, and every word thus far is true.

In the summer of 2000, I headed back to Florida for a visit with my father, Mike, and Aaron. While I was en route, I learned that my girlfriend had stolen my things and run off with another man. I was severely hurt by this and began to think about killing myself again. It had been nearly five years since I had thought about suicide, but now the thoughts flooded my mind with renewed strength. While in Florida, I decided to spend a few nights at a relative's house. I knew ahead of time that this relative had all kinds of medications stocked in her medicine cabinets. I carefully planned how I would end my life. I did not speak to anyone about it and waited until everyone went to sleep. I rummaged through the cabinets, gathered together all of the pills I could find and prepared for departure. Just before my exit, I somehow ended up on the phone with my friend, Mike, who talked me out of committing suicide that night.

30

I frequently heard whispers in my soul that taunted, "You can't turn back; it's too late! Everyone is going to burn anyway! End it! You have sold your soul to me, and you are mine! Now make every person on the face of the planet feel your pain, and indulge in everything you want. Besides, what's the point to life?"

I would fight night and day with these voices, wondering if they were my friends or enemies. Upon my return to Pennsylvania, where my mom had moved to that year, I started a relationship with my ex-girlfriend's best friend, hoping to spite her. She, like my first love interest, was also not into satan worship or Gothic metal music, but I made do.

On Halloween Day, 2000, I was hanging out with a group who believed that they were vampires. That night, I had a moment in which I thought I was going to die and had my first real vision. I came out of my body, and I saw myself lying on the sidewalk as ambulances pulled up, blood gushing from me. I was now floating above my body and could tell that my eyes were lifeless. I became extremely concerned because I realized that it was my cold, empty flesh staring back at me, and that I was gone. As I watched, my eyes changed and something came alive inside of my body that was not me. The possessed face, resembling my own, stared at me menacingly as I began to be sucked down into a dark hole in the ground.

"Rob! Rob!"

My friends were smacking me and trying to hold me up as I came out of the vision. "What's going on?" they asked.

"I....I....n-nothing, why?" I replied as I tried to act normally. Although I was freaked out, I did not want to let them know what happened for fear that they would make fun of me and recognize that I was afraid. As I was coming out of this terrifying encounter, I remember whispering "God, if you're real, don't let me die, and I'll believe in You and serve You." Needless to say, I was still alive and well, so I quickly disregarded what had happened as nonsense and continued spells and the art of witchery. I scared people just by looking at them. Once, I scared my little brother half to death just by smiling.

My desire to see the world and be different never left; it was, however, being used in the wrong fashion. I went from being different by doing crazy things no one else would do in grammar school to wearing heavy make-up and worshipping satan. Even though I felt free on the outside, I still felt trapped inside. I always had an overwhelming feeling of so much lust and so much desire inside of me that nothing in this world would ever be able to fill the void, no matter how evil I became or how much power I saw manifest.

One night as I was returning from a séance, I opened the front door to find my little Italian mom waiting for me on her knees with tears in her eyes. I knew that she had started going back to church and that she was "seeking" again, but I wanted nothing to do with her God.

"Son," she said, choking between tears. "I had no idea. I had no idea how deep into these dark things you were. I found the altar in your closet; I found your drugs, your booze, and your writings."

I was surprised that she had been going through my things but didn't really care as I had nothing to hide. I was proud of who I was at the time. "You want a medal?" I sneered, turning to leave again as I did not want to be part of an emotional scene that could possibly bring up religious subjects.

"Son, I want you to know that I've come back to Jesus. Not the legalistic Jesus but the true, free Jesus! And I've been praying for you, Robbie, I'm praying for you! Will you just give Jesus one more chance? Please!? All those years of works-based religion ruined our family; I was wrong. Please give Jesus one more chance!" she sobbed. I had already turned stone-cold the moment I heard the name "Jesus" and the sentence "I'm praying for you." In fact, when the name "Jesus" came out of her mouth, my stomach began to churn much that I felt as if I was going to vomit. My mouth opened, and out of it came a deep voice that I barely recognized.

As if from a distance, I heard myself growl: "Woman, do NOT say that Name again in my presence!" I then had to physically restrain myself from attacking and possibly hurting my own mother... because she said the name "Jesus." I quickly opened the door and ran to my car. I was nearly moved to tears as I hit my head against the steering wheel wondering how I could be so out of control. "Have I gone too far?" I wondered. "Is this it?" I thought to myself, "Why do I hate that Name so much?" This question plagued me for hours. In the midst of my deep thoughts, one idea emerged that I felt was true:

"If God, in fact, does exist, He could never forgive me for what I've done anyway, so I will not even bother questioning anymore."

Later that evening when I returned home from my confusing and emotion-driven outing, I walked in the door only to be confronted by my mom again. She was a mom on a mission who clearly was not giving up. "I have an idea, Robbie," she explained.

"What?" I asked, nervous that she would bring up the subject of God again. "It better not have anything to do with religion or God," I jeered as I glanced at her.

"Remember when we used to do, like, mother-son outings?"

"Yes," I responded.

"Well I just found out about this big outdoor music festival in the mountains," she stated, looking hopeful, "and I was wondering if you'd want to go with me this summer for a few days. It will be fun. There are going to be heavy-metal bands there!"

Now I must say, that caught my attention. But I instantly had multiple questions bombard me at the same time, such as: "Why would she be interested in a festival with heavy-metal bands? Doesn't she believe that music is of the devil, anyway? What if this is a ploy to get me into some church thing?" "You're trying to get me to some church thing! LEAVE ME ALONE!" I yelled. "I don't want anything to do with God or His so-called Son; I worship the devil!!!" With that, I stomped off to my room. Once in my room, I began to meditate in the quiet. "I can't believe she is trying this!" I thought. As I tried to calm myself down, I suddenly heard a voice speak to me.

"Why don't you go? What do you have to lose?" the voice said. "Are you not confident enough to convert all of those stupid Christians to satan?" That thought struck me like a ton of bricks.

"This is it!" I thought. "This is my opportunity to present my case and convert as many Christians as I can to the dark side!" I squealed with excitement and raced back to the kitchen to tell my mom that I would be going with her to the festival that summer.

OVERTAKEN

"Yay! You're going to go!" exclaimed my mother as I told her the news. I couldn't help but chuckle to myself, knowing that she had no idea of my diabolical plan. She then informed me that in order to go at the discounted rate that she could afford, we would have to go with a local charismatic youth group. I did not like that idea. I quickly began working on calling up friends who I knew would share my passionate vision for the festival, and sure enough, they were all for it! We decided that we would bring and sell drugs, booze and get satanic materials into as many hands as we could. I envisioned myself as "satan-evangelist" Rob. No joke. And no, you will not find that word in the dictionary!

One night a couple of weeks later, my mom and I took a drive to a "Christian night spot" to meet some of the people who would be going to the festival with us. I was decked out in all black leather, long black hair, makeup, contacts, platform boots and a pentagram around my neck.

To my surprise, a tree-hugging, hippy kind of a man who was referred to as the youth leader came over, welcomed me and attempted to hug me. I was shocked because this was the first "Christian" who had not judged me or immediately tried to convert me or cast a demon out of me.

I left quickly and continued preparing for the festival, which was just a few weekends away. Finally, the big day came. I loaded up into a van of youth group attendees, popped my headphones in and stayed to myself. I noticed them staring at me, and at one point, I think I even heard one of them chanting in a weird tongue at me. "That's strange," I thought. I remembered that as a child I was taught that "speaking in tongues" was of the devil. Now that I was "of the devil," I clearly saw that it was not because I did not speak in tongues. I was getting a kick out of scaring my fellow trip-mates when we finally pulled up to our reserved spot to begin to set up camp on the festival grounds.

After what seemed like ages, the time eventually came for me to meet up with my buddies. We quickly got down to business and began wreaking havoc. The next day, I heard that the first "Christian" heavy-metal band was going to be playing, so I decided to check it out. "That's ridiculous," I thought. "Christians can't play heavy metal! It is of the devil! Heck, drums are of the devil!"

As I made my way down to the stage, I was surprised to see people with tattoos, piercings and even some wearing all black. The band opened up with incredibly heavy songs, and I must say that I was impressed. They screamed, growled and even had whipped around their long hair helicopter-style. The guitarist was covered in tattoos, but these tattoos were unlike anything I'd seen before. They were bright and religious with depictions of scenes like the Last Supper and the gates of heaven. I honestly was not sure what to make of it, but I certainly liked the music! As the show went on I clearly saw that they indeed did consider themselves a "Christian" band because between songs they would say or scream things like:

"This next song goes out to our Lord and Savior Jesus Christ!"

I would shudder every time. Other than that little detail, I was actually kind of enjoying myself. At times I couldn't help but wonder, "How can God love them with those tattoos? If God exists at all, wouldn't He hate this type of thing?" My friends and I continued to pound the festival with satanic materials and strike up conversations about the power of the devil compared to the power of so-called "God."

A giant worship concert with nearly 90,000 people in attendance under the stars was planned as part of the grand finale of the festival. "This should be interesting," I thought when I heard about it. I grabbed a friend, and we decided to go down and check it out. Now mind you, I was linking the words "worship concert" with... well, maybe hymns or a boring session of a few a Capella songs. But no, to my surprise this concert was intense. And I'm talking ear-splitting with drums, electric guitars – and people raising their hands. People dancing. Speaking in tongues. Shaking. Wow. I had never before in my life seen anything like this! In fact, most of what I was seeing I had been taught was of the devil. Now, I was having a real identity crisis. What if everything I thought I ever knew... wasn't right? What if who I was now wasn't right? Just as these thoughts began to hit me, a man grabbed the microphone and shouted out:

"If you don't know Jesus, tonight's your night!"

I couldn't take it anymore. In one final attempt to counter what was happening in front of me, I began to mock. I mocked the worshippers, the bands, the man with the microphone... everyone. As I mocked, I was suddenly hit with a flashback of the vision I had experienced about eight months prior when I had died and come out of my body. I then heard the words that I said to God begin to reverberate through my soul:

"God, if You are real, don't let me die, and I will believe in You and serve You forever!"

My knees suddenly began to buckle under what felt like a loss of power to my entire being. I simply went limp and collided with the earth. My friend, who was standing next to me, watched as I crumpled into a pile on the ground, wondering what happened to me. There I was, big Mr. satan worshipper... down for the count. I recall my body beginning to tingle all over. I can honestly say that I thought I was dying and that I was about to get what I deserved. I expected that any moment, I would begin to rise out of my body, but instead, an intense pleasure came over me. A pure, heavy ecstasy without any drug or alcohol use whatsoever.

My thoughts raced to my day prior to this event. "Did I take anything?" I thought to myself. The answer was no. I had not done one drug or had one drink yet that day although I planned to use once this concert was over. I suddenly felt the supernatural presence of beings surrounding me on all sides. I was used to the spirit world; however I had never encountered anything quite like this before. I felt the hands of multiple beings grab my arms and hands and begin to lift them up. I watched as my arms and hands rose without any effort of my own, and I was speechless as I felt what I can only describe as a liquid river of pure love flooding the center of my being. I'm going to stop just for a moment and declare to you that even as you are reading this, you would begin to be completely overwhelmed by the same heavy Presence that fell on me that day in June 2001! Thank You, Lord! I felt something begin to churn inside of me, and before I knew it, the bubbling had worked its way to my mouth. Just then my mouth opened, and out shot the Name that I hated for so many years, the Name that the wind and the waves had to obey!

"JESUS! I believe!"

I sat astonished for a moment and then observed as out of my mouth came a cry to be a new person. My heart to be free exploded through my words! I longed to be free of all the witchcraft, drug abuse, alcoholism, lust and darkness that I had been involved in for so many years! Then came a whisper that was so soft, it soothed my soul, yet struck me as suddenly as an earthquake and caused me to tremble, and it said:

"My son, I've forgiven you." Then again! "My son, I've forgiven you. And everything that has been used against you will now be turned around and used for My glory!"

I then fell limp again as though I had just been turned inside out... and it felt incredible! As I attempted to get up off the ground and gain my footing without falling over, my friend took one look at me and queried, "Dude, what just happened to you?" with an inquisitive look on his face. I could barely speak, let alone stand! I looked at him, and all that I could manage to get out was the following:

"Dude! I JUST MET JESUS!"

"WHAT?" He exclaimed, rather confused.

"I just met Him! He's real! He revealed Himself to me!" I repeated.

Before he had a chance to say anything else, I took off running as fast as I could so I could report the events of the evening to everyone back at the camp. I must have looked like Woody from the movie "Toy Story" as I ran, wobbling and falling backwards and forwards. When I finally made it back to our campsite, the only thing I could manage to yell at the top of my lungs was,

"I JUST MET JESUS!!!"

I burst onto the scene, with makeup smeared down my face as the youth group kids looked on in fear, thinking that I might brandish a pistol at any moment! Unbeknownst to me, I had just interrupted a cute "Kumbaya" session around the campfire. For so long, I had mocked them and made fun of them, and now I was out to prove to them that I was not faking it. Right then, some of the leaders in a nearby tent heard and began to shout.

41

Overtaken

"Rob just met Jesus; Rob just met Jesus!"

All of my mother's prayers were not in vain! Shortly thereafter, some of my friends approached me, assuming that I was joking as usual. They put some drugs in my hand and told me we had business to tend to. I was amazed as I opened my hand and looked at the drugs. What I saw there was dung. Pure dung. I had absolutely no desire for them whatsoever, and I made it very clear to them that I was not joking as I proceeded to throw the drugs into the campfire. They began to threaten me, and I did not even wince. Instead, my mouth opened, and I began preaching to them, telling them how much Jesus loved them!

When I preach around the world and tell my story, I love to say that the T.D. Jakes anointing came upon me because I was going at it like I had been preaching for years! I was so radical once I converted to Christ that the new church I went to did not know what to do with me. At one point, I was out of a vehicle, and I rode my bike 40 miles each way just to tell all of the leaders in my old satanic sect about Jesus, many times with serious threats to my life. From the moment I encountered His presence, it was just as the Apostle Paul wrote in 1 Corinthians 2:2:

> "For I determined not to know anything among you except Jesus Christ and him crucified."

For me, one of the best parts of having such a radical conversion experience was finding out how God felt about me all along. I had been blinded by lies. Romans 5:8 (NKJV) states:

> "But God demonstrates his own love toward us,

in that while we were still sinners, Christ died for us."

All the while that I ran from God, blaspheming Him, causing others to stumble away from Him, He had already died for me and was passionately wooing me to Himself! That is an incredible love that cannot be thwarted by the most powerful forces in the universe.

Nothing can separate us from His love.

My Mikey

After I was dramatically awakened to the new creation reality that is Christ in me, the hope of glory, I now desired to go everywhere and do everything for this cause. Once again, I felt the overwhelming desire to stretch the boundaries and push the limits, and I was soon to find out that this, indeed, was part of God's plan! I had been walking in this new life for about five months when I received a disturbing phone call one chilly winter night in Pennsylvania. It was my best friend, Mike, my "partner in crime," one of the only people on the planet who knew everything there ever was to know about me. As we talked, we reminisced about the time we had recently spent together at Universal Islands of Escape and Sea World. We had stumbled upon a group of international visitors who happened to think that we were members of the Backstreet Boys. They were taking our pictures and singing Backstreet Boys songs to us. They began to annoy us after a while, but later we laughed about it. Right before we parted from them, I asked where they were from, which took a few tries because they didn't really speak english.

43

Finally, after some animated hand gestures, one girl stepped forward and announced, "Uruguay." I had never heard of the country and was thrilled that our pictures would be on someone's wall in a foreign country!

Mike continued to ask about me and my family. He seemed to focus on knowing how I was and if I was happy with my life and then told me he'd talk to me soon. With that, we ended the conversation. At the time, I did not realize that I would never speak to him again. Just before dawn two weeks later, I got a phone call from my other best friend in Florida, Aaron. After my mom spoke with him for a minute, her entire countenance changed, and she quickly hung up.

"Why didn't you give me the phone?" I asked bewilderedly. "What is going on?"

She started crying and looked at me and apologized, "He couldn't tell you... he just couldn't bear to tell you." My heart sank into my stomach. "Robbie... Mike's gone. *He committed suicide last night*." she sobbed.

I shrunk back in disbelief. Confused and hurting, I screamed at the top of my lungs and ran to my room to take refuge under my covers with my Bible. I took off work for days and cried and cried. I wrote his mother letters with pictures of us together that I had kept in a journal. I just did not understand. I begged God for weeks to reveal something to me. I later found out that Mike hadn't stopped using hard drugs even after I had begged him to quit. He started mixing OxyContin with other harder drugs, which proved to be fatal the night he got too depressed over a girl breaking up with him. One night, a couple of months later, I

44

had a breakthrough dream.

A small light about the size of a tennis ball appeared in front of me and beckoned, "Follow me." I ran after this light as it turned corners and flew every which way. It then stopped, and I saw a figure standing before me. As the light cleared, there was Mike. I started to cry hysterically, and I hugged   him.

"Why?" I asked.

He looked at me with sheer sadness in his eyes and between sobs, he cried, "I never knew. I never knew what it would cost the people I left behind. I'm sorry. If I had the chance to do it over, I would, but I have to face the consequences of my actions. I just wanted to tell you, when you witnessed to me a few months ago, I listened. As I was leaving my body, I cried out to Jesus and by His grace, I am saved."

I cried so hard that I couldn't speak. Then He encouraged me, "Robbie, I'll see you in the end. I promise." He winked.

In memory of Michael "My Mikey"
1983 – 2002

SCREAMING FOR JESUS

One night, I met a fine group of guys who came to perform at a weekly coffeehouse outreach where I served in Eastern Pennsylvania. I was immediately attracted to their heavy-music ministry as they traveled all over the country evangelizing through their incredible concerts! I invited them to sleep at my place that night so that they could rest well before driving back to their home state of Massachusetts the next day. We had a wonderful time of fellowship together, and a few months later I drove to New Castle, Delaware, to be with them for some of their shows. At the same time, their lead singer decided to leave the band. They asked me if I would take over as the new lead singer, and I accepted. For years it was my dream to travel in a band and scream for Jesus! I had recently been baptized in the Holy Spirit and felt endued with power from heaven to go into the entire world.

In February of 2003, I moved to Springfield, Massachusetts to join *Stratia.* I had given up what

I knew to focus on bringing secular youth culture into a radical encounter with Jesus through my new role as a vocalist. The following month, our first tour commenced in Ashford, Connecticut. Next, we stopped in Nashua, New Hampshire, and then, we were on to Boston, Massachusetts. In Nashua, someone pulled a knife on me for talking about Jesus from the stage. I loved my job and the music, and the Lord was starting to stretch me out of my comfort zone to begin preaching about Jesus during our shows.

After a fun show in Boston, we arrived in Patchogue a town on Long Island, New York, for a battle of the bands the next day featuring eight different groups. Our set was scheduled to be second to last. When we took the stage, the crowd grew so wild that I had to stop the show because someone had the whole right side of their face smashed up, and another person's nose was broken. I told them we were there for Jesus, not for them to kill each other! Although the fans were surprised to see a new singer when we arrived in Delaware, most of them took to me well.

When we arrived in North Carolina two days later, we had some trouble finding the next venue where we were to perform. We stopped at a gas station to fill up, and the man at the pump next to us glanced over at us. I immediately discerned in my spirit that he was a believer, so I introduced myself. We gave him a few of our CDs, and he gave us his phone number. We found out that he was the pastor of a nearby church.

"I'm glad God had me meet you fellows; you might need me later," he remarked just before he drove away.

"What does that mean?" I wondered. We would soon find out. Fifteen minutes later, we arrived at the "venue" where we were scheduled to play, only to realize that it was nothing more than a drug and prostitution house in Raleigh. We had no idea what we were walking into, and we had nowhere to sleep that night as we definitely knew we would not be staying there!

As a young lad gave us a tour of his house, we noticed bloodied knives everywhere. An old record player played records backwards and pot, cocaine and cigarettes were out in plain view along with porn magazines and movies stacked on the dusty tables and shelves. The stench in the dirty place almost made me vomit more than once. Dolls hung all over the walls with heads missing and knives thrust through them, posing in obscene sexual positions. A sticker at the entrance to the house boasted, "Anything Jesus did, I can do better."

We were so astonished that we decided to retreat and pray about whether we were supposed to stay there and play. As we attempted to make our way out of the backyard, our tour van got stuck in three feet of mud for four hours, so we would not be able to leave any time soon. It was obvious that God wanted us to stay and play, so I took out the little piece of paper that I had in my pocket with the pastor's number on it and called him.

"Hello?"

"Hi, is this Pastor Jose?"

"Yes it is."

"Pastor, this is Rob, the lead singer from the band that you met earlier at the gas station! We need your help! This place is *satan's den!*" I exclaimed. We gave him the address, and he and his co-pastor rolled up about 45 minutes later.

We all loaded into the house and started praying together. When the boy who owned the house heard us interceding, he took off running like a madman down the road and never came back!

Now we were left alone in this house, and kids from all over the neighborhood were beginning to arrive for the show. We proceeded to set up and play loudly and heavily in the basement. In the middle of our set, we stopped so that I share how Jesus radically delivered me from darkness. Three young people out of the 15 individuals in attendance responded to the gospel! That night, God provided hotels for us and breakfast the next morning through Pastor Jose. We thanked him, prayed together and then moved on to Columbia, South Carolina.

We arrived in Columbia to find ourselves in the local newspaper: *"Christian band, Stratia, comes Saturday night from Springfield, MA to share their beliefs in local club."*

The publicity resulted in just three people in our audience - the sound man, the drunken lady and the mocker. It was worth it, though, because we may have been the only band to ever play there that mentioned the name of Jesus. After our adventures in the south, we headed north to Pennsylvania. We had scheduled an Ohio show, but we wouldn't make it on time, so we canceled. We played in Pennsylvania at the coffee house that I had formerly helped run, so the show went fairly well. We spent the night at my mom's house before moving on the next day to Fishkill, New York, for the final show of our East Coast tour. The Fishkill organizers had scheduled us to play back to back with a satanic band, and the air was electric with tension and the presence of God as I shared my testimony and was confronted by satanists. The lead singer of the band eventually admitted that he knew he needed to turn his life over to God but that he was sure he had plenty of time to do so. After more evangelistic music adventures, we packed up and decided to head back to Massachusetts overnight. A few hours after leaving Fishkill, we drove right into a blinding blizzard somewhere in upstate New York at about 2 a.m. I couldn't sleep in our van, so I stayed awake. Another band was traveling with us, so I watched as they followed with all of the musical equipment in tow.

I started to doze off when I suddenly felt something leap in my spirit, and I jumped up to look behind us. To my horror, the other vehicle was not there. I knew instinctively that something bad had happened, so I quickly motioned for our guitarist, Matt, to make a U-turn on the interstate. Sure enough, about five miles back, we found the other band's vehicle and trailer hanging from the guardrail over the side of a mountain. I quickly dialed 911 on the cell phone and began to pray as we ran to see if they were okay.

To my amazement, they emerged from the vehicle with only a few scratches! We all huddled in the van and started praying while we waited for help to arrive. We weren't able to keep driving until daylight. Our equipment was in fair condition, but their Jeep was totaled. God was so faithful, and He protected us every step of the way.

LIFE ON MY OWN

Life on my own sounded great to me. I was now in a relationship but was struggling financially in the music scene. I had no car and was frustrated with my lack of my independence. I was slowly growing apart from my friends in Stratia, and I started to search for a good job and an apartment to live in on my own. I was tired of the lack of personal space and of sharing a vehicle and felt that I needed some independence. I decided to do a few more tours before we agreed that I needed to take a break.

It was around this time that I began to hunger after the supernatural power of God more than ever. I loved seeing young people all over the country come to Jesus, but I desired to see diseases healed and the lame walk as I read in my favorite book, Acts. Not many people during that period supported my vision. I was bored with church and bored with life.

A few weeks later, I landed a job that paid about

Life on my Own

$500 a week and found my own studio apartment nearby. I had barely enough space to turn around in – just a room with a bed and a refrigerator. I also took out a loan on a brand new car and found a church that believed in the gifts of the Holy Spirit! I was hoping that this community would spice up my life a little bit.

As I invested more time and effort into my new relationship, my job's demands grew, and my hours shot from 40 a week to 92 hours a week. I suddenly had no time to dream about ministry anymore, no time to study my Bible and hardly enough time to sleep each night. I was frequently away on one to two-week work trips from the Atlantic coast in Canada to New York and throughout all of New England.

One day, my boss hired a tall, creepy guy in his mid-20s and assigned him to travel with me. He had been raised a Christian but dabbled in some of the same dark things that trapped me in the past. His name was Teddy, and despite his poor influence, we gradually came to be good friends.

I dragged him to church once in a while, but the more he came to church, the more I compromised my convictions as well. For a couple of weeks, I found myself trapped in a world of lies and darkness again, falling into pornography and surrounding myself with things from which I was powerfully delivered two years earlier. I told the Lord I was sorry for dabbling in the things of darkness again and rekindled my prayer life. This brought me a little peace, but I was still troubled.

In addition, I was having issues with my landlord,

who was constantly on my case. I had to share a bathroom with five other men, and I did not like it, so I had been quite irresponsible with the bathroom privileges. Each morning, I dreaded rolling out of bed and waiting for Rodger, the nice old man who lived on the other side of the wall from me, to take his shower. Then I would quickly claim the shower before the crack addict down the hall could get to it. After three months of working 90 hours a week, no sleep and hating my living situation, I started to have horrible anxiety attacks and finally broke down and became extremely sick. I was out of work for a while, in and out of the hospital, with a fever every day that spiked to 105 degrees. When I recovered a few weeks later, my bills were piled sky high. Then the hospital bills began to flood my mailbox. I knew deep inside that God had something better for me, but for some reason, I kept trying to do things on my own. I thought that if I just worked and strived hard enough, with God at my side, I would be able to pull it off by myself.

Each day, I thought about the big dreams God had put in my heart - dreams to travel the world and see lives changed through the power of the gospel. But it wasn't happening. Instead, I found myself standing at stop lights on the Interstate with a box of items that I needed to sell on commission. I felt utterly humiliated that I had allowed myself to stoop to this level. Men and women would sneer at me, make obscene gestures and threaten me.

One day, I approached a man who clearly needed healing in his body, and I knew that if I did not make money that I would not eat that day. As I neared his window, he motioned for me to go away. I inched closer, and he began yelling at me. "I don't want to buy your stupid stuff!" he shouted. I could not take it anymore and threw my box to the ground and ran over to the man.

"Sir, I don't care about selling you anything! Jesus loves you so much and wants to heal you!" I shouted. "Will you let me pray for you?"

"Go away!" he yelled as he hobbled quickly to his car. "I don't want anything you have to offer me!" I was heart-broken. I was sick and tired of being sick and tired. That night as I lay in my bed struggling to sleep, all I could see was the face of that man and thousands of other faces that he represented who needed the hope that is only found in Jesus.

I finally fell asleep in the wee hours of the morning, only to be awoken at 3 a.m. by a smoky stench hovering in my room. I thought I was just dreaming, so I rolled over and tried to go back to sleep. I had to be at work in two hours, and I wasn't about to be disturbed now. As soon as I turned over again, I heard a slight crackling sound. Just as I sat up in bed, the loudest, most frightening noise pierced the air in my damp little studio room in the middle of winter. The fire alarm blared, and I knew that if I didn't get up, I could be moments from my death!

I quickly grabbed my guitar, Bible and wallet, and prepared to jump from my two-story window. I knew that I might break my legs, so I decided to check out the hallway. I touched the knob to find that it was warm, and I cracked open the door and peered into the hallway. Black smoke and flames were billowing out of an apartment two doors down from mine, directly next to a Christian brother's room. I darted down the stairs and out of the door into the cold, icy air. People were already lined up on the sidewalks. I took a moment to catch my breath because the smoke I inhaled was thick, causing me to cough and nearly choke. I scanned the crowd outside for my Christian friend, Wayne, but he was nowhere to be found. I threw some rocks at his window, hoping to wake him in case he was sleeping through the fire. I knew he would perish if he were still inside. When I saw flames explode out of the window next to his, lighting up the night sky, I knew I had to do something. I saw another man yelling for help and preparing to jump from his window.

I quickly darted back into the building, ran to the second floor knowing it could mean certain death, and violently banged on Wayne's door as hard as I could. The flames were nearly scorching my clothes. He finally answered the door as he had somehow slept through the catastrophe! As I pulled him from his room, his walls were engulfed by smoke and began to collapse. We made it outside safely with only minor coughing.

The firefighters broke into the last room to extinguish the flames. The man who rented the room at the end of the hall was nowhere to be found. The blaze had started when the man, Joe, fell asleep on the couch while smoking drugs.

The next few days were very solemn for me. The incident had left me searching and somewhat shaken. I started to read my Bible more often and looked into some missions programs abroad. For some reason, I especially desired to go to New Zealand. The only place I was not interested in going was to South America because I had grown up in Florida and struggled with a root of racism in my heart against Latino people. The months turned into a year, and a new burden increased in my heart for the mission field. As the days went by, I started to have more and more interest in missions and foreign ministry. I began praying for missionaries and continued searching for mission trips to join.

Shortly thereafter, the girl I was seeing at the time was leaving for a three-week trip overseas. Global travel and serving the Lord was the desire of my heart, and I wished I were the one leaving. Although I was a tad jealous, I would now have extended time alone with Him to clearly hear His voice and seek Him concerning the next step.

During the next few weeks, I decided that something had to change. If Jesus had come to give us abundant life, why was I not experiencing that life? I recalled the story of Gideon in the Bible and knew that if God could get a hold of just one person, He could change nations. I found myself steeped deep in a spirit of fear, not knowing what it would look like to leave my current life behind to follow the call of ministry once again. I had nearly died trying to uphold life on my own, and I was tired of not following the dream that God had put in my heart. Over the course of the next two weeks, I kept asking myself if I would be willing to do anything for God. I almost felt as if the Lord was asking me this question. After a few days of pondering, I finally responded with a big "Yes!" I suddenly felt that it was time to leave my "together" life for the unknown. The thought scared me half to death but excited me at the same time. I determined to go for it.

Too Much Sunshine

Clearly some major changes were coming soon in my life, and now that I was actually taking the plunge, I was looking forward to what the future held. The studio room where I still lived had a nice maintenance man who would frequently talk my ear off. One day as I was praying about the next step, I ran into him while coming back to my room. We talked for a long time, and I started to feel God's heart for this man. I sat and listened as he recounted me the tragic events of his past. My stomach churned as I heard his story. I started to tell the man that God loved him and that I desired to become a minister and see people's lives change   for   God.

"If I were young, oh, the opportunities I would take up!" he confided in me.

"You think I should go for it?" I asked. He stared at me with a look that seemed to say, "You know what you're supposed to do." I thanked him, ran back to my room and immediately started packing all of my things. I left the maintenance man a book along with a note telling him that God had a wonderful plan for his life. My rent was month to month, and it was the end of the month - so I was free!

When my girlfriend returned from her trip, we talked and mutually agreed that our relationship was not God's best for either one of us and decided that it was time to move on. After a conversation filled with tears, we parted ways. A few days later, I was on a Greyhound bus with only a guitar and my backpack. I did not know what awaited me at my destination, but I sure couldn't wait to find out!

Thirty long hours later, I arrived in Orlando, Florida. I had the opportunity to minister to many people on the bus. Once I arrived in the New York City bus terminal, I even handed out Bibles from my backpack stash as people lined up to receive them along with prayer! I felt that I was already moving in the right direction. I called my dad on the way and asked him if I could stay with him for a while. We hadn't seen each other in a long time, and our relationship was still very unstable from the divorce years earlier. When I arrived, I found myself very emotional and feeling vulnerable. No car, no job, no real relationship with my dad. Only good old friends and an awesome church to attend that I knew about from my previous summer visits. I had spent all of my childhood in Florida, but this would be my first time living there in six years.

My father had left the faith years ago and now suffered from alcoholism. As you can guess, our relationship was filled with immediate conflict, and I longed night and day for him to return to the Lord. With a new wife and other children to tend to, my dad was a person I felt I no longer knew. Everything went okay for a little while, but I quickly realized that I could not be in the situation long. I decided to take a job at a local pizza joint that I could walk to. I intended to save up just enough money to attend a Missions and Evangelism school in New Zealand. Since I only earned around $100 a week, it proved difficult to help pay my expenses and save anything. It would be close to two years before I would have enough to go. It wasn't long before things went sour. My dad grew tired of finding me praying in my closet and hearing me preach at him and his wife non-stop. I foolishly thought that if I told them there were demons in their house, they might come to Jesus. I began to warn them of the demonic activity I was discerning in the home and in their lives, and that only made things worse.

I began having trouble at the pizza parlor where I

worked at as well because I just couldn't seem to properly make the food. One morning my boss, Vinny, who was straight from Italy, yelled, "You have a higher power! Why the h*** don't you ask Him for help!?" The next day, I was fired. The situation with my dad became even more tense until one day, when things finally came to a head.

As I tried to reason with my dad about his alcohol problem, he completely flew off the handle. I had never ever seen my father this angry in my life. He screamed that I was foolish, chasing missionary dreams and that I would amount to nothing.

"God is not going to help you or send you anywhere!" He growled. He then added, "You're useless, and you're going to do the same thing to your family that I did to ours!"

"I cannot receive this for my life," I responded as I choked back the tears. It was time for me to leave, but where would I go? I began to question if Florida was indeed the correct move or the wrong timing. I was physically scared of my dad that night, so I packed up and called my uncle. He arrived early the next morning while everyone was still sleeping. I left a long heartfelt note for my father and told him that I hoped someday we could resolve our relationship and that I was sorry I didn't meet his expectations.

My aunt and uncle let me stay with them for free for a while, and I got a job landscaping with one of the ushers from my church. My uncle taught a Bible class in the church, and my aunt was involved with the missions program. I felt much better in this environment.

Life on my Own

I sat everyday listening to my hillbilly boss talk about how we are God's children and deserve the best the world has to offer as he sucked down whole sticks of cheddar cheese with his crooked yellow teeth and southern accent. The best cars, the best houses, the most money, etc. At the moment, I did not care if I was poor, as long as I was preaching the gospel somewhere. I also could not understand why he was only paying me a measly $7 per hour if he really felt that way.

I soon became one of the worship leaders in the church youth group where I attended. My good friend from middle school, Aaron, found out that I was in Florida and was looking for a church to attend. He was overjoyed at my salvation experience! I brought him to church shortly thereafter, and he was filled with the Holy Ghost, and we began leading worship together! Aaron and I shared the same kind of relationship that Mike and I always had before his death. I was so happy to have a good friend again since I missed Mike so much and felt the same way about Aaron.

Now Aaron was quite the character. His nickname was "Balls" because his last name was "Baltusis." Don't even ask. Honestly, he always amazed me. He could be a funny airhead and an annoying goofball one minute, yet very spiritual and full of wisdom in the next minute. I looked up to him a lot, and we shared so many great moments together. Aaron and I were always seeking the Lord together, which was a big difference from when we were younger. He stood with me and prayed for me even while I was a satanist.

Shortly thereafter, we went to a nationally televised 'healing crusade' in Orlando which featured a famous minister. I had never been to anything like it, so I was curious to see what it would be like. I watched in awe all night as God used this man to miraculously heal people in front of me! I didn't know how he operated in such an anointing, but I was hungry to find out! I wondered that night if God would ever be able to use me in a similar fashion.

About half way through the meeting, the minister pointed down to the audience and announced, "You! With the dog tags around your neck! Come up here!"

I looked around, and it did not take me long to figure out that Aaron and everyone around me was staring at ME. I looked down and suddenly remembered the dog tags I had put on earlier! I made my way up to the stage with eyes on the television cameras that were staring back at me. The man motioned for me to come to him, and when I approached him, he proceeded to ask me a question.

"Has God ever used you to heal somebody?"

"No!" I responded, shaking.

"Well, He's going to right now," he prophesied. Before I could say anything else, he called forward a lady who needed a healing in her hips so that she could walk correctly. Right then, he yelled "Lay your hand on her head, son!" I did what he said without a second thought. The instant that my hands touched her head, I felt an electric current shock my body, and we were both thrown in opposite directions to the ground. I had no idea what happened, and when I opened my eyes, I saw the lady on the ground in front of me praising God!

61

I tried to get up, but much like my conversion experience, I could only make it to my knees. There I knelt in awe of what had happened, and I watched as the lady stood up with no more hip problems and walked away praising Jesus. Everyone erupted into applause, and I finally managed to pull myself off the stage floor. I carefully made my way back to my seat under a very heavy presence of the Lord.

"Dude, that was awesome! What did you feel!?" Aaron exclaimed.

I had no words. When I finally managed to reply, I could only ask, "Did I look stupid flying through the air up there?" I tried to explain what I felt but to this day words still cannot describe it. God was really taking me to a deeper place in my relationship with Him during my stay in Florida. I had received what I needed for the next part of my journey.

One day a couple of weeks later, my youth pastor approached me and asked me if he could speak to me in his office. I agreed and followed him. As we sat down, he proceeded to tell me something that would change the course of my life as I knew it.

BREAKTHROUGH OF THE CALLING

Pastor Ryan stared at me straight in the eyes with a rather amused look on his face.

"Rob, it looks like you're going to South America!"

Within a heartbeat of time, my emotions swung from confused to happy and then upset because I did not want to go there. In fact, at this point, I had already been saving for three months to go to New Zealand. The pastor explained that an anonymous person had just paid for an upcoming mission trip in full with my name on it. I was stunned. No one had ever done anything like this for me before. I quickly wrote a letter to the anonymous person thanking them, but I never did find out who it was. If you are reading this – **Thank you!**

Now, the race was on. I went back home and prayed and asked God why He was sending me somewhere that I didn't feel called to go. I arranged another meeting with Pastor Ryan to find out more about my destination. He had mentioned Ecuador previously, and I wasn't too thrilled about that idea. It seemed too close, and I wanted to go as far away as possible. It turned out that the Ecuador trip was full, and I was to go to Uruguay. I was shocked since I knew nothing about Uruguay other than it was pretty far away.

I went home and reflected as I tried to remember where I had heard of the country before. Then it hit me. The group that Mike and I had met years before at Universal Studios had been from Uruguay. It then occurred to me that Mike, who was no longer on the earth, and I had our pictures on someone's wall in Uruguay. I realized that all these years later, it was a prophetic sign. This was the time the Lord was calling me to my first foreign country where I would be able to share Mike's story and pray for those considering suicide. I was excited, but I had a long time to wait since it was only February, and the trip wasn't until October.

Now I understood why God had brought me to Florida. He wanted to open a door that otherwise would not have opened! I soon returned to Pennsylvania to spend some time with my mom. She had been through another rocky divorce and needed some support. I ministered to her and then told her of my mission opportunity, which she supported 100 percent. As the year progressed, however, I lost sight of the vision for the mission trip and decided to go after one of my long lost passions, cosmetology. In case you haven't noticed yet, I was very easily distracted and lacked focus. I wanted to ensure that I would have a career if God suddenly decided not to use me anymore. Although I did not yet truly understand the character of our Heavenly Father, I was on a journey of discovery. The year seemed to fly by, and I enrolled in cosmetology school just a few months before my scheduled departure for Uruguay.

I kept myself busy putting on evangelistic concerts in the area as well. I frequently wore white and black makeup, lots of leather and started a subculture outreach. I did see some fruit, but most of the secular youth would not come to church for the shows, and most of the local Christians were scared away. On one particular night, a rather reserved church group came to my show. The idea was to reel in local kids and then share my testimony.

One minute into my first song, the church group took all of the chairs out of the church and decided to congregate in the parking lot to pray against me. When I was done with my show, I spoke to some of the other local youths about Jesus, and then I went out to visit those congregated in the parking lot. A few older women shuddered and ran away from me. I had taken my makeup off and began chatting with some from the group. They said that they respected my ministry but could never come back again because there was too much spiritual pressure. I knew that demons were being put to flight as I gave my testimony, and I understood that the atmosphere was quite intense. I was somewhat disappointed by their lack of support, but I understood that this type of ministry was not for everyone.

Finally, October rolled around, and I hid from the mission team that was trying to contact me because I no longer wanted to go. I had forgotten what God had done for me back in February of that year in Florida. My life seemed to be coming together with my career and goals, so I changed my mind. A few days before the trip, I was awoken by a dream. A red sky was stretched out over my head, and

Breakthrough of the Calling

I saw a mighty harvest taking place in nations all over the world. I saw groups of angels with sickles, and they would sing a song to the Lord and gather wheat from the field. I woke up in a cold sweat as I knew that the Lord was telling me that I had to go. I packed my bags and prepared to head to Miami to meet the mission team.

I had never been en route between land and air for 15 hours before, so I wasn't sure what to expect. Just to clarify the geography, the country of Uruguay is south of Brazil on the eastern coast of South America with Argentina to the left. As my mom brought me to the airport on that crisp fall day in 2004, I knew another chapter was beginning. I could feel it in my bones! Next stop - Buenos Aires, Argentina.

Fuego y Gloria

I could not sleep at all. To this day, I travel extensively and still can barely sleep on planes. Too much excitement! After what seemed like forever, we finally touched down in Buenos Aires. It was glorious to me! We had a long layover there so I checked everything out and bought some souvenirs. I noticed some strange cups that were made out of goat hooves that the residents used to sip tea. I didn't know one lick of Spanish, so I just browsed the many gift shops in the airport. Hours later, the time arrived to board the plane for Uruguay. We finally arrived in Montevideo, the capital of Uruguay, during a beautiful spring day. "Wow, it's kind of chilly here!" one of my teammates said. "It's Uruguay, not Chile!" I quipped, trying to be funny. They didn't laugh.

And He Unleashed Me to the World   **Rob Radosti**

As I looked at my surroundings, I saw fields, rolling hills and palm trees. It wasn't exactly paradise, but it felt very different than home for sure. You could immediately feel a very quiet, tranquil, but heavy state of solitude in the country. As we made our way out of the airport, I was stopped by young boys who wore hardly any clothes as they begged for money and food. I was told not to give them anything, but I just couldn't help myself. As we strolled throughout the city and down the beaches, I saw many high-rises and old European style buildings. We arrived at a small church in the nearby town of Canalones that was packed full of people waiting to feast with the group of Americans! I enjoyed my first Uruguayan meal of bread, cheese, rice and Coca-Cola. In Uruguay, the people drink gigantic bottles of Coke – all day long.

As I walked down the dirt roads of the little pueblo, I saw everything ranging from large gated houses to small wooden shacks on the same roads together. The next morning after a good night's sleep, we took a four-hour bus ride to Mercedes, Uruguay, where our mission project would start. After only about an hour into the trip, one of the tires on our bus blew out. We were stuck in the middle of Uruguay in a field with nothing but a Frisbee and lots of fresh cow manure to play in. We tossed the Frisbee back and forth for some time, and then I was offered traditional Uruguayan Yerba Mate tea, which was a strong tea sipped through a bombilla, a metal straw, out of a gourd. I have to admit, I was skeptical at first because I thought it was a street drug! We finally made it to our hotel. Each morning, we split up into three teams: a construction team to build a church, an evangelism team and a children's team.

I joined the children's team, and we went throughout

67

the villages with a portable audio system, singing songs and performing skits. We handed out Bibles door-to-door and offered to pray with people. One day as we were ministering on the side of the road, a pastor from the other side of town showed up to check us out. He had somehow heard about us. We got along well, and he invited me to come and preach at his church that Wednesday night. I was so excited for the opportunity! The day arrived, and I excitedly gave my testimony at the church with the help of a translator.

After my message, I had the opportunity to share Mike's story and pray for all of the youth. Many were touched powerfully by the Holy Spirit. I even felt like the Lord told me that a certain young girl was going to have a powerful radio ministry that reached into all of the Uruguayan villages. I had never prophesied before, but I decided to release what I felt the Lord saying. She began to cry and said in broken English that this was her ministry dream! To this day, she is a leading voice of a powerful radio ministry in the nation of Uruguay.

That was it; I was hooked. I felt like I was finally being unleashed into the calling that I knew was on me from the moment that I met Jesus years earlier. To top it off, I began to understand Spanish at an accelerated rate. I was wondering how this was happening, and I realized that it must be a gift of tongues at work in my spirit. In the 10 days that I was in Uruguay, I began to preach in Spanish without ever having studied it except for briefly in the seventh grade when I skipped nearly every class. I received more invitations to preach and minister, and I was already making plans to return to Uruguay the following year and continue my ministry there. When we were boarding our plane home in Montevideo the following week, I actually had tears in my eyes. You might say I almost cried for Argentina! When I arrived home in the States the next day, I was instantly down. Everyone was doing the same things, working the same jobs, and no one seemed to understand what a life-changing experience I'd had. God had changed my heart toward the beautiful Spanish people, and I could not wait to go back!

THE NEXT FRONTIER

I'd been home for just a few weeks, and the hope of returning to Uruguay was shortly disappearing on the horizon as I got busy applying for jobs while the bills began to stack up. I had missed too much school and would have to reapply, which was something that I did not want to do at the moment. Within a few months, I felt that I needed to get out of the country again and really seek the Lord as to the next step for my life. I began to experience a previously unknown serenity when I traveled, and I longed for that peace again. I found very cheap tickets to Zurich, Switzerland, at the same time that a great Christian rock festival was being held there. I decided to go for the weekend to attend the concert in February of 2005.

On a snowy day, during takeoff, the plane went down nose first and hit the runway as we lifted up. Apparently, they did not properly de-ice the turbines, so they now had to find us a different plane. I was praying hard the whole time! I finally flew to Europe where I made some good friends at the festival over the weekend that took me to the Swiss

Alps for the night. The gorgeous peaks and pristine beauty of the countryside was a beautiful backdrop for a wonderful time. Believe it or not, I ran into someone from Uruguay all the way in Switzerland. I felt more determined than ever to return to Uruguay for an extended period of time. When it was time for me to leave the airport in Zurich, I bought a train ticket to Bern the Swiss capital by the French border, where I and ended up staying in the flat of an acquaintance. I woke up early in the morning to catch the two-hour train ride to Zurich. I couldn't speak a word of Swiss-German, and unlike Uruguay, I had not picked up any of the language. I had no idea what train was headed which direction, and no one seemed to speak English, so I picked one and hopped on, hoping that it was the right one. Incredibly, it was. I had heard that the Swiss rail system was rated the best in the world, but I certainly questioned that when my train broke down just ten minutes shy of the airport. I raced to another substitute train and ended up dashing into the airport with only minutes to be on the plane. I had enjoyed Europe but was ready to plan my return to South America. My heart ached for the miracles and power that I had seen in Uruguay. Although I was carrying the same anointing, I had never quite seen it manifest in the same way as when I stepped into my destiny in October 2004.

The Return

Around mid-August, I landed a job at a gas station to begin saving for my next trip to Uruguay. I talked with my church leaders about it, and they supported the trip. I was really praying and seeking the Lord about what to do in Uruguay when I got a revelation. I remembered that nearly two years earlier, I had received a prophecy while visiting a church in North Carolina that I was chosen by God to "reinterpret for this culture the things of God," and the word 'YWAM' appeared in there somewhere. It then dawned on me that I had never checked to see if YWAM, or Youth With A Mission, had any opportunities in Uruguay. I guessed they did not, but to my surprise, I was wrong. As I looked at the website, I found a missions base located in Rivera, Uruguay, across the street from the Brazilian border. They offered a "Discipleship Training School" once a year. I became so excited that I was beaming and had to call a friend to ask them what they thought. They said that it bore witness with their spirit, which was important to me because they were known to be very accurate prophetically.

I bought my plane ticket to depart on November 2, 2005. I had not set foot on Uruguayan soil for 13 months. I was becoming more and more excited as the time drew closer. However, when October rolled around, I again became distracted, just like the previous year. God was really doing a lot with me at my local church, and I was going to miss everyone. Even so, I was set to go to Uruguay for a month and reluctantly prepared the best that I could.

I again found myself on an 11-hour plane ride to Argentina, and I could not sleep at all or even listen to music. I could not do anything but sit and wonder what God was going to do over the next month in Uruguay. It began to hit me that I was traveling completely alone. No group, no team, just the Holy Spirit and me. Mind you, we were an incredible team! I tried to read some books, but I couldn't focus. This plane did not have a GPS tracker, so I couldn't see where I was in the world. I was very upset about this because this held my attention for hours. When I arrived in

Argentina for a stopover, I was so tired that I attempted to sleep in the terminal. When that didn't work, I just sat and waited anxiously to board the plane to Montevideo. What seemed like days later, I finally boarded, only to arrive in Montevideo exhausted and to realize that I could not locate my ride. Hordes of people crammed the terminals holding signs written in Spanish, such as "welcome home" and others. In a daze, I became momentarily overwhelmed and just wanted to turn around and start flapping my wings back to the USA. Just then, I heard a voice.

"Roberto, Roberto!"

I laid eyes on a very tall man that I had never seen before. I wasn't sure if I was in danger or not, but he knew my name. He told me in Spanish that his name was Pastor Alejandro and that he was sent to come get me because my ride could not come. I felt relieved and followed him out to his car. It was so hot outside, and it was only the beginning of spring! We zoomed straight down a strip of road that seemed to be about 5 feet from the ocean in a car that would not have even passed inspection in the 1940s in America.

We strolled into a section of the Boulevard Artigas in the center of the city and screeched to a stop in front of "La Oficina Nacional de la Iglesia de Dios en el Uruguay." I was told this would be my quarters for a few nights, and I was led inside to meet a wonderful host family. They took me to the zoo and taught me many things about Montevideo and the country's culture in those four days.

Excerpt from my Journal Entry –
November 2, 2005 Montevideo, Uruguay

"Once I arrived, I went outside and strolled around the brick streets, observing the cuteness of the little brightly colored buildings squished together, the colonial Spanish architecture of the villas and the giant "U" fountain near the government building. Towering palm trees at least 40 feet tall adorned Boulevard Artigas while the sidewalks below bustled with people in need. The beauty of the countryside contrasted sharply with the needs of the people. Cross-dressed prostitutes stood on nearly every corner, and I watched as a fight broke out right in the city center.

I saw some homeless couples lying around gulping heavy liquor, and I could hardly cross the street without nearly getting killed. I wondered if these people even know that Jesus died for them. I learned that my host had to save about a month's salary just to buy himself a pair of shoes! And this was the man whose entire family was serving me! I am overtaken by love, yet at the same time grieved for the condition of the land. My mind cannot even comprehend the need! I retreated for the night to write, reflect and pray. I have learned so much my first day."

I knew that my stay with the host family in Montevideo was limited to a few days, so I began searching for a place to stay in Mercedes. As I was inquiring, I found out that there was to be a mighty international crusade starting November the 12 in none other than the small Uruguayan town of Mercedes, the exact location where we were the year before. I found someone to stay with and decided to serve at the crusade. I was ecstatic, especially when I learned that this minister had prayed for Benny Hinn before his worldwide ministry was launched. I wasn't quite sure what was going to happen next or even what God wanted me to do on this trip. I just knew that I had to go. After more downtown tours in Montevideo, I was ready to depart for Mercedes. I returned to my room and prepared for my bus trip the following day. Some friends from last year's mission trip planned to meet me at the bus station and take me to stay with them at their house.

When they arrived, the first thing they did was to point at my tattoos and criticize them. I just ignored their remarks and tried to continue our conversation, but to no avail. They could not seem to get over my tattoos. Needless to say, the four-hour bus ride was quite awkward, and I was glad when we finally arrived at 2 a.m.

The next morning, I was hungry, jet-lagged, and ready for a big breakfast and a nice hot shower. I could nearly smell the aroma of fresh eggs, bacon and pancakes in the air! I jumped up only to find out that Uruguayans do not really eat breakfast except for a small piece of bread or some milk. Boy, was I disappointed! Traditions were very different, and I just had to adapt. I was missing home already, but I comforted myself with the thought of a nice, hot shower. When I asked where the showers were, they pointed me to a small, cold concrete cell with a water spout. I shivered though my shower, wondering what I had gotten myself into. To make matters worse, my hosts had a pet "paloma" or pigeon that kept pecking me – during my shower, as I got dressed and even when I went to sit down and eat lunch! Everyone was staring at me strangely, and one person remarked that Uruguayans do not shower in the mornings. I attempted to lighten the mood by telling them that I was hungry and that if their pet pigeon did not stop pecking me, that I was going to eat it for breakfast the next morning. However, I was the only one laughing at my own joke.

They brought out large plates of meat-filled pasta with what seemed like stale bread. I am not a pasta fan, so I told them maybe I would take a walk to a store to see what they had there. They were then very offended by me, and I could tell because the host's grandmother made a couple of sarcastic remarks about my tattoos and ridiculous earrings and walked away.

Needless to say, I was off to a rough start this time around in Latin America. That night was church, and apparently, I was fashionably loud. I had spiked-up blonde and brown hair, big purple sunglasses, Express jeans, big earrings, shiny shoes and a black Pop Star jacket, topped off with some expensive cologne. As I walked into the church, people just stared at me and I only got a few "holas." The pastor greeted me, and the service started. I was asked to share, and I gladly got up and told the church how I longed to be there for months, and I missed all of them very much. Later, someone told me that it was extremely disrespectful to wear sunglasses while inside or when someone was talking to me. It was a rough night.

The next day, I was so hungry that I decided to head to a local market to see what I could find. To my surprise, I found some tubes of Pringles, American potato chips. I was so excited that I bought them and hid them in my bag. Later that night, as I was stuffing my face with chips, my host family walked in on me! I had not eaten much of the food that they had offered me, and they were upset. They felt like they had let me down as hosts, and I apologized. I rotated nights between other families' homes, and my time in Uruguay began to improve. We sat around fires until 3 a.m. most nights, talking and learning about each other's cultures. All of the guys wanted to hear about American women while all of the women wanted to hear about American guys. It was odd but fun.

Finally, the healing crusade was about to start. I was hoping that this would propel my trip ahead in the right direction. I dreamed about how they might call me up to share in front of thousands of people and about how God might use me to heal diseases and pull folks out of their wheelchairs. I was sure this was my big break.

THE FACE OF ADVERSITY

My stay in Uruguay was certainly taking a different twist. I had come expecting much publicity and expecting to minister in a few choice churches, yet it didn't happen. The crusade started, and I finally got to meet the minister that I had heard so much about. He seemed to be a great guy, and we had fun times of fellowship. As the crusade started on the first night, I watched as hundreds of people packed into the event. I had never actually seen a real live crusade on the mission field before, so I enjoyed the evening as I carefully watched how the speaker operated in the anointing. Up to this point, I was mainly involved only in street ministry and outreach, but I had preached at a few select youth groups and small tent revivals back in America. I did venture out over the next few nights to minister in the streets, but I was surprised at how unwelcome my outreach was when it came to the young Uruguayans. They mocked me, and some of them even ripped up the Bibles that we were handing out. They seemed stone cold to the gospel message. I was now gaining the understanding that the country was steeped deeply into humanism and atheism.

One day as I was speaking with some friends, I was casually invited to give my testimony at a Baptist youth group. It wasn't the large crusade I was hoping for, but I was thankful to have any opportunity at all to finally minister! When I arrived, the senior pastor immediately left the building as soon as he saw me! I figured I would make the best out of it, so I started by greeting the youth pastor, and then moved to each young adult. There were about three of them in the church! Before I knew it, I was preaching to them through a translator that I had met a few weeks back; it seemed that for some reason, I wasn't able to speak Spanish the way I could the year before. However, she was struggling with some of the words, and it was very frustrating to have to stop and keep repeating myself.

After my message, I decided to lead the group in some worship. Instead of using hymnals, I told them that God wanted us to worship Him from our hearts and enter into His presence where there was joy. I took an acoustic guitar and began to strum the song "Praise Adonai" as I sung in Spanish along with some other worship songs that I had learned. When I peeked to check on their expressions, their faces stared back at me blankly. I proceeded to welcome the Holy Spirit and began to pray softly in tongues. The next time I dared to look, people were lifting their hands and closing their eyes. I was ecstatic! I thought that we just might be having breakthrough in the Baptist church!

I joined the group for food after the service as I got everyone's contact information. They were really precious people, and the youth pastor, who just happened to have the same full name of another Uruguayan pastor I knew, invited me to come back and minister the next time I visited.

79

The Face of Adversity

I thought it was amazing! I had turned down an invitation to another Uruguayan city by the Argentine border that night to be at the Baptist Church's youth group because I felt it was where I was supposed to go.

I spent many days writing, praying and pondering by the side of the Rio Negro, which means "Black River," and it is aptly named! If you put your hand even two inches under water, you can't see it. Even so, I swam in it.

Despite my original plans, I never went to the border town of Rivera to visit the YWAM base. My visit to the small town of Mercedes was rapidly drawing to a close, but I felt aimless and felt that I did not accomplish God's purpose for me. I was frustrated that I did not see more fruit from my time there.

Why was I not walking in my destiny when I knew I was called to it? It reminded me of Adam and Eve in the Garden of Eden. They were called to walk with God but chose to be distracted and disobey. I made a solid decision to impact as many people as I could in the time that I had left. I was able to do two powerful radio interviews in those last few days and declare hope and freedom to the nation of Uruguay, and then it was time to go.

This was truly the hardest moment yet. I couldn't wait to go home because the entire month had been so rocky; however, my heart also ached at the thought of leaving behind the country that I loved so much. My closest friends showed up at the bus terminal for a sentimental good-bye. Fighting off tears, I boarded the bus headed for the eastern part of the country. In case you haven't noticed yet, yes, I am a pretty emotional guy.

When I finally arrived in Montevideo, I was picked up by Pastor Alejandro and taken to his place for the evening to await my flight. I did not want to be there; I did not want to be anywhere. The time came to go home, and I headed to the airport. I had a hundred thousand thoughts racing through my mind, and knew that I would have the next 16 hours of travel to ponder the events of the past month. One thing that I already knew for sure - this was not my idea of a successful ministry trip. No, not at all.

REGRESO

I was in deep thought concerning the events of the trip as I awaited my turn to board the flight to Miami at the airport in Montevideo. I recalled how I had sensed God's heart to pour out His presence in the nation. I sat and stared at the clouds and the sunset over Buenos Aires again as we flew over the city. I scrolled through hundreds of pictures I had taken of my trip along with video footage of the ministry crusade and architecture in Montevideo. This kept me busy for a while until I drifted into sleep almost all the way to Miami. Nothing could prepare me for what happened next. We touched down in Miami, Florida at 4:45 a.m., and the Homeland Security welcome was intense, not that I'm complaining. It was so hot in Uruguay that I had bought the local street clothes and shoes to stay cool and to blend in culturally. I happened to wear these vestures on the plane in order to be comfortable as I traveled. However Miami officials looked at me with suspicion. I had no sooner received my passport stamp when an officer approached me, asked me if I spoke English and sternly commanded me to follow him.

I proceeded to obey and held my breath as he uttered, "I hope you don't have another plane to catch because you will be here for a while." I tried to tell him that my flight to New York left in 45 minutes, but he brought me into a small room and disappeared.

During a long interrogation session, my bags were completely searched as I removed, unfolded and repacked all of the contents. He finally released me, but just as I was leaving, another officer saw what he thought were drugs in my pocket. I'm not sure how he got that impression, and it turned out to be only a few loose pesos. After a good pat down, I was finally free to go. The authorities had made it clear that they thought I was using my role as a missionary to cover drug smuggling. They had even thumbed through and shaken out my Bible while telling me that they were sure I had probably hidden drugs in it. Just then, I was almost to the metal detector when I realized that I hadn't seen my camera since shortly after takeoff just before I had fallen asleep. I then realized that I couldn't find my watch or earrings, so I decided to check my bags. I was devastated to discover that I had been robbed. My digital camcorder and camera, along with all of my memory cards and photos, two watches, earrings and other small things were nowhere to be found.

I sat on the plane back to New York in utter depression. I had no pictures to show anyone from my trip only my memories. When I arrived in New York, I was happy to see my mom and my brothers who had come to meet me. We exchanged greetings and headed out. The air outside felt like Antarctica to me, and I bundled up.

Regreso

I had missed my loved ones very much, but I already didn't like being "home." I felt homesick for my new country. I explained many of my adventures and mishaps, and we caught up on events. Going back to work after the trip wasn't easy, and after a few days, it almost felt as if I had never left. But over time, I began to enjoy working with our small local youth group again. There were about 20 of us, and good things were happening. I even started an intercessory prayer meeting which met once a month, called "Battlefield Earth," where I brought everyone up to date on news of the persecuted church around the world. We prayed for the nations, and my heart was so filled with passion for ministry, but I felt that no one else really shared the same vision that burned within me.

I had a lot of fun continuing to play music and help lead at our Christian coffeehouse on Friday nights, and we started to bring in ministries once or twice a month that would help draw local youth to hear the gospel. On one of these evenings, we were hosting an evangelistic illusion show designed to offer an opportunity to respond to the good news of Jesus. The ingenious show drew a large crowd. It was such a success that we decided to have them back often because of the impact their show and message seemed to be having! As our ministries became more connected, I noticed that even the illusionist's assistant, Millie, started coming to our youth group meetings on a regular basis. For a girl that had swords stuck in her and appeared suddenly in a cage of fire, she seemed very interesting. I was told that she was on many medications and was frequently in and out of mental hospitals. What was even more interesting is that when she showed up, she brought hordes of people from local partial hospitalization programs who were responding to the gospel by the droves! I was quite impressed but still kept my distance. Honestly, I couldn't wait to leave for Uruguay again, and much of the time, this consumed my thoughts. I desired to return in March, and I was constantly praying and asking the Lord to open the door for me to do so. I felt in my heart that I wanted to move to South America, and no one else around me seemed to understand. I decided to bide my time and make the best of it.

DECISION OF A LIFETIME

I had been home from Uruguay for a few months and frequently felt badly because I didn't visit the YWAM or JUCUM or Juventud Con Una Misión school in Rivera like I had promised. I felt that God had ordained it and began to wish that I had checked it out. I had received an email from a friend in another part of Uruguay who told me that the school had prepared for an American to visit, but the guy never came. They thought it was awful, and this only made matters worse. I responded by agreeing, "Oh how terrible...."

Needless to say, I quickly got back in contact with the YWAM base at the school, apologized and told them that I was praying and fasting about what God wanted me to do next. I was working with a roofing company in the middle of winter, and all I wanted was to be back on the mission field, seeing lives radically changed. I did get the opportunity to love on and minister to my co-workers, but my heart was still elsewhere.

I was feeling very down until I finally bought a plane ticket to return to Uruguay on February 20, 2006. I now knew that if I was going to serve on the mission field, I didn't want to attempt it again without formal sending and training in the culture. Upon making this decision, I decided to talk to our Wednesday night pastor, who was personal friends with Loren Cunningham, the founder of YWAM. To my delight, he thought that the school would be the best thing for me and even agreed to support me financially!

I finally decided that I would attend the YWAM Discipleship Training School in Rivera, Uruguay, and I would leave in two weeks. I was not able to raise sufficient support before I left, but I was determined not to let that stop me! I had to rely completely on God. I realized that I wouldn't have a way back to the USA, but I was ready for the adventure. No one around me seemed to worry too much about it, so I didn't either.

Six days before I was due to leave, my step-grandma fell and broke her arm, so I spent my last few days transporting her to various doctor's appointments. I knew I was going into a whole new world of serving, and I was happy for the opportunity to be a real blessing. I couldn't wait to minister to the Uruguayan people again.

I had just recently found out that at the time, Uruguay, along with Cuba, had the highest suicide rate of all Latin American countries. Most of the suicides were by adults, and they also boasted the highest alcoholism statistics.

My heart yearned for the mission field, and I felt ready. I wanted to pack as little as possible yet wanted to have some things to offer the poor street children when I arrived. I didn't want to chance getting anything stolen this time, so I bought a tiny MP3 player and downloaded all of my favorite CDs onto it. Music was of utmost importance to me, but the last time I had gone to Uruguay, I had carted all of my CDs with me, which was over half the weight of my luggage! I was learning. My flight this time would go from New York and then to Miami directly to Montevideo. I wasn't looking forward to the hot weather there, especially since the city where I would stay on the Brazilian border is the hottest in the country. The normal February temperature is around 100 degrees Fahrenheit. We had a huge blizzard the week before I left home in Pennsylvania, so I enjoyed the beautiful white scenery.

I started to have second thoughts, but I fought through them. I was ready to go. I thought of the bird flu that was spreading at the time, and how if it spread rapidly within the next year or two, all of the countries would close their borders, and I would never get home. I thought of things that could go terribly wrong with friends and family while I was away for who knew how long. I had to clear my mind. Two nights before take-off, I had a dream of everything around me being destroyed, but my angels kept me standing until everything was restored. I knew that I wasn't alone and that it was time to turn the page.

CULTURE SHOCK

The wheels of the American Airline's jetliner touched down on Uruguayan soil to a steamy summer day in Montevideo on February 21, 2006. It took all of my strength to haul my bags up onto a cart and through hordes of people in the airport. Little street children continually attempted to pickpocket me and my bags on that hot, sticky day. I waved down a taxi and headed toward the bus station. I was exhausted and found a nice little hole-in-the-wall for 180 pesos or $7.00 a night. I unloaded my gear as I looked forward to getting some sleep! First, I hopped into the cold concrete shower and observed the lines of little ants marching on to war as I washed myself.

I woke up starving at noon the next day. I had no food or drink with me and a small budget. I decided to walk to a nearby market to see what I could find. I picked up some cereal and water and went back to my bug-infested motel room. I still had about 10 days before I needed to head to the YWAM base, and I had arrived early, hoping to make some new ministry connections in the meantime.

Culture Shock

That night, I was invited to minister at a youth retreat. I preached my heart out as I shared my testimony at the retreat, and I even learned to dance "La Cumbia," which is a very popular dance style in Uruguay and Argentina, after I was done! It was a lot of fun – that is, until I was led to my sleeping quarters. I wasn't much for "community living," and I wasn't thrilled about sleeping in a hut with 10 other dudes who I did not know. Twenty-one years of independent and comfortable American living was enough to make me wonder how I was going to fare at the YWAM school. I was certainly hoping that the accommodations would be better than this. The next night, I found a better hotel room for only a dollar more, this time without bugs!

I knew I didn't have money for another night's hotel room, so I started praying. Thankfully, the next day, someone connected me with a local pastor who lived in Montevideo. I was told we would get along great because we had similar testimonies, and I was happy to hear that he also sported some tattoos. That afternoon, the pastor arrived to pick me up, and we instantly connected.

It turned out that he ministered to heavy-metal musicians in Uruguay, which was right up my alley. He had come from a past of drug dealing and darkness as well. His church was just starting out, and they were on fire. He introduced me at their next service, and I was suddenly traveling around Montevideo doing a mini-revival tour. At one church, the glory of God fell harder than I had ever seen before as I ministered, and people began to fall all over the building. At least four people were delivered of demons that night, and I was amazed. I instantly felt the passion of Jesus burning in my heart and knew that this was my call without a doubt. One young man named Jorge happened to come in off the street that night and heard my testimony. He was so touched by God that he came to talk to me afterward and gave his life to Jesus. He was a famous local nightclub DJ and had been involved in all sorts of alternative lifestyles. Now, he wanted freedom. Jorge was instantly delivered that night and became a radical believer! We became good friends, and I plugged him in to one of the local churches. God was already doing great things in Uruguay! I really felt at home, but then it was time for me to attend the YWAM DTS in just a few days. I was planning to take an eight-hour bus trip through the night. I was excited to start yet another new adventure. I said my goodbyes, gave hugs and hopped on the bus. What would the coming days look like? I could not wait to see!

Arrival

I awoke as the bus pulled into the Rivera station on the Brazilian border in northern Uruguay just in time to exit so that it wouldn't drive away with me again. At 5 a.m., it was nearly pitch black. Yawning, I plopped down on a bench with my bags to wait. I thought that somebody would at least hold a sign with my name on it! After 30 minutes, I finally decided to try to call someone with my prepaid Uruguayan cell phone that I had bought in 2005. It was very expensive to use; the only thing it was really good for was text messaging, which only cost one peso per text. I tried to communicate that I had arrived and was waiting, but the line seemed to be bad, and I didn't receive much of a reply. Frustrated, I sat back down on the bench and waited again. I was tired, cranky and was starting to become very annoyed by a cheerful character sitting next to me. He slowly sipped his Yerba Mate gourd, the traditional Uruguayan tea drink, and hummed as he inhaled the morning air. He glanced over at me a few times, but I just glared back. About 20 minutes later, he turned to me and asked if I was Robert from the USA. "Si! Para Juventud con una Misión!" I replied.

"Bueno!" He responded as he helped me with my bags and pointed me toward his car.

"You could have said something 45 minutes ago!" I thought to myself.

After four miles through winding dirt roads and hills, we arrived at the "chacra" of YWAM Uruguay. Once I saw the facilities, I understood why they were using the word "chacra" or farm. I was shown to my dormitory, which consisted of a small wooden shack filled with bunk beds and a few shelves. I stared in disbelief, suddenly feeling like I had just signed my own death certificate. At that moment, I wished I were back in Montevideo preaching at revival meetings and staying in hotel rooms. I wanted to cry. The school was still two days away from starting, and I already wanted to be done.

After a short nap, I told myself that it was time to go and make some friends. I met the leaders of the school, and I honestly couldn't help but laugh at them as they seemed to be a bunch of poor, directionless kids. I know that my reaction was horrible! I needed to allow Holy Spirit to do a lot in my heart, but this was not the way I was hoping it would happen. It didn't take me long to realize that I was being stared at left and right, specifically because of my tattoos and earrings. With every passing millisecond, and I'm not over-exaggerating, I was becoming more and more depressed. I felt like I turned myself into some kind of foreign legion.

I then got wind that there was an American at the school who was serving as a leader. I just had to meet him!

My ears were tired of Spanish, and I felt sick every time I heard it. The following morning, I ran into a tall, slender man with reddish hair who stood with both feet facing the opposite directions. He sported a bright orange Texas sweatshirt, blue jeans and boots. "Hi, my name's Darin!" he announced with a thick Texan accent. Well, here was the American who I couldn't wait to meet. My heart sunk in disbelief. "I'm not going to have anything in common with this dude!" I thought to myself. I tried to be friendly as he began to tell me all about his calling to Uruguay, and how he and his wife met in Colombia, married in Texas and more.

Things took a rough turn for me as the school started, and my only outlet became my journal and my MP3 player. Our schedule included waking up every morning at 6 a.m. sharp, drinking warm milk and meditating on scripture for an hour. Then we were to sit in the little wooden classroom for four hours, eat lunch, work for two hours outside in the heat and then partake of dinner, followed by more prayer and worship meetings in the evenings.

As the school progressed, we worked with churches in Brazil every weekend and did plenty of fun, evangelistic outreaches in the streets. This was right up my alley, but I still didn't like the instructors and the fact that my freedom was in the hands of other people. The schedule seemed fierce, and at times, I felt like a slave. I very much looked forward to Mondays because they were our "free days."

Culture Shock

I would spend most of them exploring Brazil, just on the other side of the border. I had bought a bike, and I would ride by myself deep into Brazil. Americans need a special visa to enter Brazil, but I did not have one as they were very expensive. One time, I was caught by a police officer quite a ways into southern Brazil. He asked for my passport and then told me to get back to the other side as fast as I could, or he would arrest me. This became a ritual.

As for school, I ended up in "discipline" so many times that I began losing my one free day a week. I was definitely learning a lot, including Portuguese and more Spanish. Before long, problems arose between me and the Brazilians as they were very loud pranksters and didn't have much of a sense of personal privacy. At various times, I would go looking for something of mine, such as food, clothing or other random items, only to find it missing. Then, along would come one of my Bolivian or Brazilian brothers, nonchalantly sporting my sandals, clothing, or even rubbing their tummy because the stolen food that they had eaten was delicious. Although it took me quite a while, I had to learn that this was not a felony but a culture!

I loved to be alone. I popped on my MP3 player and jammed out to Christian metal music any free second I had. Everyone who even attempted to listen to it was a bit freaked out, except for the Chileans. Darin, the leader from Texas, actually ended up being a very` close mentor to me. I started to allow him to pour into my life, and it began to crack down the walls of hurt and offense that I had built up over the years.

Journal entry – March 21, 2006

"Here's God's way: Basically give up everything you've ever had, have and hope to have. God is really dealing with my heart, and it's horrible to my natural mind. My heart has been wrong this whole time, and I've been viewing a blessing as a curse. Brokenness is what God needs; after all, He cannot form a sun-dried sculpture. God has shown me my pride and my rebelliousness, and I repent of it. I've caused so many problems, it sickens me. It's a good thing God has me here before my public ministry starts. I really needed a heart cleaning! God knows what's best, and He wasn't joking when He called us to war. The effect I've had here so far has certainly been negative.

Something worth mentioning at this point is that a YWAM DTS has two "phases." The theoretical phase at the school location lasts about three months, and the practical phase, normally a specific outreach in another culture or country, lasts about two months. The time was drawing close for us to begin our practical phase, and I was growing more excited every second! The leaders were discussing the possibility of Morocco for our practical phase, which would last the months of June and July. I had no clue how I would pay for it, but I suspected that if it was God's will, it was His bill.

After all the sessions were completed, we were told that the destinations for the practical phase were Morocco and Peru. I was open to either one but preferred Morocco as I had never been to Africa before. Because I only had a few donations coming in each month, I wasn't sure how I would pay for it.

Culture Shock

Before I left the States, I had found 20 close friends and relatives to sponsor me for $20 a month, but only three had been faithful to their pledge. As I sat dreaming about Morocco and asking God how I was going to go, my friend Pablo walked up to me and announced, "Dios va enviarte a Bolivia." Translation: God is going to send you to Bolivia.

At about 5 feet, 5 inches tall with only a few rotten teeth and a body that suffered terribly from epilepsy, it wasn't easy to understand Pablo when he attempted to talk. I gave him a lot of credit because he chose to leave his family to come to the school while knowing that he had random seizures and frequently needed hospitalization. I had trained my ears to be able to understand him, and I didn't like what he was saying. I didn't even take one moment to imagine that he might be correct; instead, I automatically rejected his message.

"You'll see!" he kept adding. I didn't know what God was up to, but I was sure that He didn't want me to go to Bolivia. I was convinced that the Moroccans needed the gospel much more than people in Bolivia.

CULTURE SHOCK, REDEFINED.

Just a few days later, our little group of 12 people boarded the bus to Buenos Aires, Argentina, where we would connect to a two-day bus ride to Santa Cruz, Bolivia. The Moroccan trip had ironically fallen through, and the Holy Spirit confirmed to me that Bolivia was indeed His will. We arrived in the beautiful city of Buenos Aires, Argentina, on May 31, 2006.

Seemingly hundreds of skyscrapers, restaurants and tons of nightlife captivated us, and I thought, "Now, this I can handle!" After spending the whole day out on the town with Darin and our little group, we headed back to the station to board our bus to Bolivia. As I looked around at those preparing to board with us, I noticed that they looked very different. Their faces were clearly more indigenous than those I had previously had experience working with. They sported bright psychedelic blankets, little top hats on their heads and babies on their backs. They were speaking the Quechua language, so I was rather intrigued. We would all be on the bus for the next two days, so we tried to get comfortable. Just as we were departing, a man hopped on the bus, started singing songs on his guitar and asked for money. After the authorities took some time to get him off the bus, we were off! Every time that we stopped to pick up more passengers in central Argentina, someone would hop on trying to sell special herbs or something interesting.

The drivers often wouldn't even bother kicking off the vendors but just ignored them. Through the night, we stopped for bathroom breaks and food, and I noticed that after we were all boarded, one of the drivers hopped outside. When I looked out the window to see what he was doing, I observed the locals talking with him as he took whatever they offered him in exchange for a ride. He snuck them into the bottom of the bus, babies and all, where the luggage was kept! Note to self: Do not keep expensive things in your luggage as it is transported underneath buses in South America. I watched this happen all the way through the "pampas."

The next morning and afternoon, the landscape started changing. It went from pampas to isolated mountains and rugged cliffs in the distance. I nodded in and out of sleep as we drew closer and closer to the Bolivian border. Finally at about 9 p.m., we arrived at the border. I could see a large gate with some rocks in front of it flanked by dozens of people being stopped by border patrol while crowding to get into Argentina. Just then, a Bolivian security guard crawled on to the bus and started to check passports and travel documents. Some people did not have the required paperwork to cross, and I watched in disbelief as they were thrown off of the bus right there at the border. A million thoughts started racing through my mind. "What if I get thrown off? What if they don't like my documents or the fact that I'm American?"

Just then, Miguel, who was from our group, was called off the bus. Apparently, they didn't like his documents. He was allowed to return after a lengthy search and the payment of a small fine. When the man got to me, I handed him my passport, swallowing hard. "What will they think when they see that I'm from the States?" I thought. They shrugged, stamped my passport, and moved on.

My relief was short-lived when I heard word that there were rioting groups protesting outside who had heard there were Americans on the bus. Just then, they began pelting our windows with rocks! I ducked down in my seat as far as I could as I imagined a large rock flying through the window and breaking my nose or worse. The next stop was the immigration office where we all had to get off the bus and stand in line to get our visas and fill out papers. As we got off the bus, I was shocked to see the drastic and major change in scenery. There where little stands dotted across the brown dirt with indigenous people selling their crafts and barefoot small children who were barely dressed running around near midnight. As we single-filed into the offices and started to fill out our papers. Afterwards, I traded some my money for Bolivian currency and climbed back on the bus. Finally, when everyone was back in place, we were on our way for the seven-hour journey to Santa Cruz de la Sierra. As we entered Bolivia through a town called Yacuíba, I watched the little houses and mountains go by while I finally drifted off to sleep. Just after midnight, I was awakened as the bus screeched to a halt.

I asked what was going on, but to my dismay,

nobody knew. The driver flung open the door and stepped outside. He radioed back and forth on his walkie-talkie and then turned around and yelled "Todos afuera!" Translation: "Everyone outside!" I started to panic.

As we all lined up to exit the bus, I stared out the windows at the pitch black sky, wondering what could possibly be happening. We were told to grab all of our luggage from underneath the bus, so we waited in line under the stars there in the middle of the mountains. For me, grabbing my luggage meant carrying three bags, two suitcases and a backpack. I was into my fashion, and I did not travel light. As I recovered my things, I glanced around to see if I could figure out what was going on. Nothing could prepare me for what I saw next.

To my horror, I saw giant blocks, broken glass and people gathered in groups brandishing weapons and blocking the bus from going any further. "We're all going to die," I thought. "This is it." Knowing I struggled with a negative mindset, I resorted to praying in tongues. Just then, the bus driver instructed us to huddle together and move forward. "Move together?" I thought. "He can't possibly mean walking...." But that was exactly what he meant.

We found ourselves in the middle of local protests and riots with cars on fire and flipped over, and gunshots being fired. The rioters had blocked all of the major roads in Bolivia. Scared to death, we prayed and set off on foot. It took us about three hours to walk a mile since we had to drag all of our luggage on our backs. Before long, everyone from the bus except the ten people in our group had disappeared. Towering cliffs bordered thick jungles on both sides of the road, so we could not see anything. We climbed steep mountain roads and navigated sharp curves as we passed several hostile groups who just stared us down as we crawled by. Darin and I made it a point to keep our mouths shut so that we would not give away our American accents. We finally came to a point of utter exhaustion and dropped everything to rest on the side of the road.

We had not seen signs of civilization for hours. Our only companion was the dim moonlight as it weakly attempted to crack through the fog. I snapped a picture of our little group huddled on the side of the road but then quickly put away the camera after I was told that the hills had eyes.

Sometime around 3 a.m., we stumbled across a man driving a small station wagon. We weren't sure how he had made it through the barriers. He asked if he could help us, so we agreed to go three at a time with our luggage until we were all to the other side of the riots. According to the driver, this would take about another 30 minutes. We had all been walking for hours, and we felt that we absolutely couldn't go any further. As he opened the door, we loaded up our luggage, and I was one of the first to jump in. "Lord," I remember praying, "If this is a wrong move, then let us know right away because I cannot even think straight right now." Just as he turned the key, the front tires both blew out. I immediately jumped out of the vehicle, knowing that we were in danger, and the man sped off on screeching rims with half of our group's luggage, never to be seen again. Thankfully, my things weren't in there, and neither was I, or I probably would've disappeared as well.

Culture Shock, Redefined.

At about 4 a.m., we started to see light! We ran up ahead to find that we were approaching a town called Camiri. Little did we know that this was the center of all the riots. We carefully crossed a bridge full of groups of angry, violent people tipping cars and shooting weapons in the streets. I was so tired that I grabbed my pillow out of my bag and collapsed on the corner of a street near the center of the mobs. After sleeping in the middle of the road surrounded by fires and violence, we were awakened to hear that there was an empty bus nearby where we could sleep so that we would not be in nearly as much danger. We gladly accepted the offer, remembering that the bus driver had said that he had arranged for another bus to pick us up on the other side of all of the commotion. I had no idea how he would find us. I was hoping this bus was the one that he had been talking about. However, to my dismay, this bus had been stuck in the same spot for four days. We were told that the passengers who were in it had left on foot days ago. I couldn't believe it. I couldn't fall asleep no matter how hard I tried, thinking of how long we might be stuck in the middle of Bolivia with no transportation, food, water or means of survival.

I prayed, "Okay God, if You know what You're doing, now's a good time to prove it!!" After sleeping about an hour, at 7 a.m., Darin and I decided to go exploring to see just how bad it was and to look for any other routes out of the area. But I shouldn't have gotten my hopes up. After walking about 20 minutes, we still saw trucks and abandoned buses lining the highways. We were told that some of the people had gone into the mountains in search of water because they had been stuck in the same spot for a week. "They would never allow this kind of nonsense back in America," I thought to myself. We turned around and made our way to the downtown part of Camiri, which consisted of a few small buildings and gas stations. Every kiosk or store and gas station was out of water and food and closed. We found a vendor from a nearby pueblo who was selling bananas, and boy, was I thrilled to eat one!

We headed back to the bus to report our findings to the rest of our group. They all agreed that the best thing to do was to continue walking. Again, I was not very happy but didn't want to chance being stuck in that same spot for another week, so we were off. We walked about another three hours in the hot sun. Finally, we collapsed on the side of the road on top of our luggage, which was a quaint little bed for the moment. Although it was winter, the tropical sun was beating down on us so heavily that I thought I was going to pass out. After sleeping on the side of the road for a few hours, we awoke to see something approaching us from a distance.

It was a bus! Hundreds of people flooded toward it from every direction and jammed it full. They wanted 50 bolivianos per passenger. Most of us had no money, so we waited and prayed. At 3 p.m., we saw a familiar logo coming down the highway, "La Veloz del Norte." I couldn't believe it! It was the bus that they had sent to find us the day before! As we hopped on the bus starving, dehydrated and exhausted, I noticed something written on the door of the bus: "Deus e fiel." That is to say, "God is faithful" in Portuguese. A few hours later, after a long, much-appreciated and air-conditioned ride, we arrived in Santa Cruz de la Sierra, Bolivia.

IN THE THICK OF IT

We wandered through the Santa Cruz bus station, dizzy and smelly. Finally our contacts found us as we were squeezing our way through the hordes of people. A half an hour later, we pulled up to the YWAM base of Santa Cruz. We were all so relieved that we had a bed and that we were still alive that we jumped in victory as we marched through the doors! The people inside thought that we were a little "loco," but they had had no idea what we had been through! I could barely eat and wash myself before crawling into a real bed. The next morning, we all slept in, then woke up and had worship. I was very antsy because we were now in yet another new country, and I could not wait to check it out. Curiosity had always been part of my DNA as I traveled. We would be here for three days to rest before moving on to the church we would be working with in the area. Everyone on base waited expectantly to hear the grueling tale of our journey. People from all over the world had come to this base from Korea, Argentina, Colombia, Chile, Brazil, Paraguay, Peru, the USA and many other places. In fact, I was excited to find that more than two people spoke fair

English! The facilities at the base were very nice with delicious breakfasts, lunches and dinners, not to mention much more freedom than our base in Uruguay. A few other students and I trekked off to explore Santa Cruz. The bus stop was right in front of the base, so it was quite an easy system to figure out. As we stepped onto the bus, we realized that it was actually a chicken bus – small, sweaty and overcrowded. So overcrowded, in fact, that you either were pick-pocketed, pecked by a chicken or ended up dead from claustrophobia. About a half an hour later, we arrived at the city center. We spent the whole day exploring Santa Cruz and checking out the restaurants and shops. A few days later after we had rested up, a large jeep arrived, towing a trailer to transport us to the church where we were working. We all squeezed into the jeep together. At least there were no chickens pecking us this time!

When we arrived at the church in the local barrio or town, it was raining, and we unloaded all of our wet luggage into a pile on the concrete floor of the church. The church reminded me of a concrete stadium, except not quite as big, more like an auditorium with no doors or windows, just open air. There was a small church school attached. We were going to be hosted by several families for the next four weeks in groups of two. Miguel from Montevideo, Uruguay, and I were together, so we grabbed our things and climbed into the Jeep to meet our host family. Amazingly, they only lived about eight blocks from the church. They owned two giant pit bulls that got to know us after a few days. We were sleeping in a small concrete room; however, the accommodations were not bad at all. I slept better than I did on my small bunk in Uruguay, so I was happy.

Over the next four weeks, we were told that our

assignment was going to be ministering to young children. "Great," I mumbled under my breath. I wasn't a very big fan of kids at the time, and we were going to be working with the children of this small church school as well as street children. I soon learned that the government was threatening to shut down this school because they wanted to outlaw Christian education in Bolivia. Our little group met at the church every morning, worshipped and ministered to the children in the school. I was always getting into trouble. I couldn't pay attention during worship and prayer as my mind was always floating off in the clouds.

We spent time with the children, counseling them and performing skits and dramas that showed them in their language Who Jesus is and what He did for them on the cross. It really was a blessing and a great experience. Even so, I especially looked forward to every Monday, which was our free day. I would spend it doing the same types of things that I did in the States but for much cheaper. For example, I would eat out three times, get my haircut, go grocery shopping and more for under $30. I was probably the only student who had his own stash of food in our entire missionary group. I remember back in Uruguay when I was told that we had to wash our clothes by hand, and I secretly snuck them to a laundromat every week. Until I got caught, that is. The family who we were staying with had a small washer and dryer unit. I was so excited! Bolivia was beginning to grow on me. For two months, we ministered at all of the services, special presentations for the children, dramas, worship, and to top it off, we also went to the streets at night with dramas and music. We went to the worst park in town with all of our skit makeup, ready to evangelize the streets. Although drug deals were going on all around us, we took our places and waited for the cue of the music to start. A crowd gathered around us to watch the skit, and then I preached my testimony of deliverance from darkness, and we talked to the crowd and prayed with them. My calling was begging to be unleashed from inside of me, and I suddenly began to feel alive.

VIVA COCHABAMBA!

After four incredible weeks of powerful ministry in Santa Cruz with just a few glitches, our time had drawn to a close. We were preparing to move on to another town for the remaining four weeks of our practical phase in Bolivia. We said our goodbyes to all of the great people that we had met and made our way onto the bus that was leaving for Cochabamba. About two hours into our journey, we crossed the line to the indigenous side of Bolivia. A beautiful tapestry of jungle and mountains filled the landscape as far as the eye could see. Halfway through the trip, however, our bus squeaked to a halt, and we were suddenly faced with reliving the nightmare from weeks before once again. We were stuck yet AGAIN in the middle of Bolivia!

I didn't even bother to put on a good act but just exited the bus with my journal and went up into the surrounding hills to write. I wasn't sure how long this stop would last, so I tried to make myself comfortable. The road was in very poor condition, and reportedly, this time the cause was construction on the only mountain road running through central Bolivia. "Why couldn't someone have told us before we left Santa Cruz?" I thought. As I sat and journaled, I quickly became uncomfortable when I realized that the native people were squatting to take care of their business in the river right next to me. While this might seem like an exaggeration, the people just relieved themselves wherever they were, babies on backs, top hats and all! I was shocked. I made my way back to the bus because some very funky colored bugs were starting to hold a dance party in the air and dive-bomb my face. Thankfully, this incident was not nearly as dramatic as our little excursion in Camiri weeks earlier as we only had to wait about four hours.

Journal entry – June 30, 2006
Somewhere in the middle of Bolivia

"You're not going to believe this. Yep. The second time in one month! Right now, I'm sitting in the midst of a breathtaking valley, surrounded by towering mountain peaks and lush green jungles with cascading waterfalls. Gorgeous, except I'd rather see it from inside the bus. We're stopped in a place even more inconvenient than the last time! We left Santa Cruz at 7:30 this morning; right now, it's about 3:30 p.m., so we're only about two and a half hours from Cochabamba. The church had an awesome "goodbye" service for us, complete with dinner, last night. I was a little emotional, but not terribly."

We arrived in Cochabamba that night at 8 p.m., July 2, 2006. As we pulled in through the mountains to the city, I could see the statue of the Christ standing tall and lit up on top of the mountain with thousands of lights in the valleys below. The atmosphere clearly felt very different here. Now

Viva Cochabamba!

July is winter in Bolivia, but in Santa Cruz, it was very hot. In Cochabamba, however, it was freezing at night, and I had brought no blankets or extra clothing to keep warm.

We met our hosts at the bus station and proceeded to a pastor's house where we would be spending the night. That morning, our group awoke to make sandwiches as we ministered to the poor, then settled down to discuss our time in Santa Cruz. We talked about the positives and negatives and how we had each personally grown. Later that day, we set out to see the stunning natural beauty of Cochabamba. Although the landscape was a bit browner than Santa Cruz because of desert conditions, the views were breathtaking nonetheless!

After a few days of rest, we were transported to the church where we would be working. Before we left, the pastor's wife gave me a beautiful traditional Bolivian camel's hair blanket to keep me warm. I was very thankful!

Upon our arrival, we were shown to our quarters, and I was to share a room with three other young men from my group. Our living space consisted of a small, cold, concrete room about the size of a large walk-in closet. My personal space was a small, flat hay mat with questionable stains on the hard, cold floor and nothing else. I couldn't believe it. My back hurt just looking at it! After setting down our things, we were given a tour of the church premises. The old church was situated on a corner, enclosed by large metal fences on all sides and watched by a guard dog. The pastor and his family lived in a small house behind the church, and small concrete meeting rooms adjacent to each other behind the church completed the property.

As we entered the sanctuary, I suddenly got the feeling that we were not going to be very welcomed there. Don't get me wrong, the pastor and his family were very nice, but I picked up on a lot of religious spirits. The church had gained no new members in more than five years and most of the members had been there for 20 years or more. They were not very open to new ideas, but the pastor desperately sought change.

Surprisingly, a small drum set and a broken-down electric guitar stood in the sanctuary, which the pastor fought tooth and nail to keep. The enclosed sanctuary reeked of mold. I wasn't thrilled about this assignment in the least. The next day, we decided to break up the atmosphere by saturating the sanctuary with praise and worship, speaking in tongues, and anything else God wanted to do to unleash freedom in the place. I grabbed an acoustic guitar and just start praising and prophesying over the church. We all entered into God's presence and started to march around the sanctuary and proclaim freedom and victory for this church. We began to bind demons and anoint everything with oil, and suddenly, the atmosphere shifted and grew very heavy. The following is a true account of what happened next as documented in my journal.

Journal Entry - July 6, 2006

"So much can happen from one day to the next; I don't know where to start. Yesterday after I wrote, we were in the sanctuary worshiping and anointing everything when my friend Pablo was apparently attacked by a demon! It looked like he got electrocuted twice, and then he fell. I caught him and let him gently down to the ground. His face

was locked in terror, his mouth open wider than possible, and a high-pitched sound came from his mouth. His eyes were bulging out of his head, and then they turned blood red. He lay on the ground bubbling and foaming at the mouth, and his blood-red eyes rolled back in his head. We all started to pray and cast out the demon. Just then, his face started to change. All of the skin on his face started to turn gray and crack, almost giving the appearance of scales. One of the girls felt something exiting through her hand, and after that, he responded. The pastor called 911, but we tried to explain that it was a demon. He was eventually rushed to the hospital, but they could find nothing wrong with him."

We all had trouble sleeping that night. Our entire group felt as if we were on the front lines of an invisible battle. At about 4 a.m. that morning, my roommates and I were awakened to a loud thump on the ceiling, then the sound of large flapping wings. We were a bit startled, and all jumped up as we looked at each other inquisitively. Suddenly, we heard one of the girls from our group screaming at the top of her lungs "Darin, Darin! Ayudanos!!" (Translation: Help us!! Darin and Carolina, the leaders of our group, stumbled out of their rooms and dashed across the property toward the yelling to see what the ruckus was.

Apparently, this young girl and her friend from Brazil had gotten up to go to the bathroom, which was across the property. I ran with my roommates across the property to help, and when we arrived, we heard the girls describing what had happened. They reported that when they got into the bathroom, they heard sounds coming from just outside the door. When they looked through the foggy plastic window on the bathroom door, they saw the outline of a dark figure. One of the girls quickly locked the door and asked, "Who's there?"

They heard the figure clearly respond, "I'm an angel," in an evil, almost seductive, tone. At this point, they decided to swing the door open quickly and run in the opposite direction. We saw them burst through the door just as we ran across the property to see what was happening, but *no one was there*!

They told us that as they swung the door open, the figure just vanished and left them confounded in their fear. We were all flustered over the situation and began praying. Only the pastor and his family were on the property in their house with their own bathrooms. When the pastor was told about it, he could not fathom demonic activity on his property and stuttered, "It must've been the cat!"

Don't get me wrong, I'm a cat lover, but I was pretty sure I didn't want to come into contact with this breed of cat ever again! Even so, I was a bit skeptical of his assessment of the situation. I thought about how the property was guarded carefully with tall fences and an attack dog that didn't even bark once throughout the entire incident.

After we all calmed down and spent some time in prayer, we finally went back to our rooms to try to get some more sleep just before dawn. It took me only moments to fall back asleep, but the moment that I did, I found myself in a horrible nightmare. I dreamt that I was being chopped up with an axe. Then the scene changed, and I was alive again, only to be tied up on a cross. Men in black, military uniforms with masks on appeared and violently shouted at me to deny my faith in Christ. "NO!" I screamed. They yelled repeatedly as I kept screaming, "No!"

The leader walked up to me and mockingly said, "This is where your faith has gotten you, fool!" He open-fired a machine gun throughout my body, leaving me hanging there lifelessly. I woke up sweating and nearly hyperventilating. I restlessly dozed off again near 6 a.m. and fell back into the same dream. This time, I was tied at the hands and feet. The military men had a giant saw that they used to cut through my body, starting at my abdomen. I saw my organs begin to fall out, and I woke up.

As I sat up praying and sweating, one of my roommates got up at the same moment. He asked me for prayer and said that he also had a horrible dream. I sat astonished as he recounted my entire dream back to me in detail – *except it was his dream, too!* Needless to say, as our group gathered later on that morning, nobody wanted to stay in Cochabamba!

We knew that we were needed, so we decided to jump in whole-heartedly and trusted that God would take care of the thick darkness that surrounded us. We began to worship in the church, teach evangelism through drama and art., and prepare to lead a Vacation Bible School for the street children. Many of the church members had never heard of evangelism! Obviously, a lot of them rebelled against the pastor because they did not like change and wanted everything to stay the same. Our next week wasn't as eventful, my back grew accustomed to the whole sleeping arrangement, and we became closer to the people.

It was now time for the annual Quechua Feminine

Conference when all of the native women from the surrounding mountains gathered together to worship in the Quechua language, cook their food and just enjoy each other's company. We were not told that this particular cultural group bathes in rivers with their clothes on instead of taking showers, and they were not accustomed to using a toilet. It would have been very helpful to know these little tidbits of information beforehand.

The next few days were challenging, to say the least. For days, the air was filled with various strong odors and loud chattering that sounded like hundreds of squirrels. One day, the women wanted to make us a special, traditional meal. One thing you must know about me – I hate soup. I watched in horror as they plucked living chickens, boiled vegetables and prepared to make giant pots of... soup. I was starving, but I could not eat that disgusting soup. I waited to see if there was anything else from which to choose. I was so excited when I saw fried chicken being passed around and grabbed a few pieces and went to town! After about four bites, I tasted feces. I instantly knew what it was, and I wasn't about to keep eating it. I asked Carolina, and she told me to stop saying that it contained feces because she was already in the middle of eating the chicken as well. I begged her to tell me what I was eating. She finally answered me quietly as she didn't want her girls to hear. I was eating horse intestines!

I started to gag and quickly dashed outside. Once there, I found a stand selling hamburgers and sweet-potato fries. I could not have been happier! I had been warned not to eat the street food in Bolivia, but I was so hungry that all common sense left me. I grabbed the food, inhaled it and returned to the dinner nearly unnoticed. After dinner, we had a time of worship, and I found myself feeling very nauseous as I prayed over all of the Quechua women.

Once I finished, I retreated to my little concrete room and lay down on the stained hay mat, feeling terrible. Before long, I was suffering from cold sweats and passing in and out of consciousness. For the next two days, I was terribly ill with food poisoning while the others who ate the horse intestines were not!When I finally recovered, it was almost time to move on to our next assignment. We fed the poor and did street dramas, and I spent my free day exploring the restaurants and taking a gondola up to the Christ statue, which was exciting.

Our next stop, just up the mountain and a few miles away, was the Anglican church. Upon arrival, we clearly noticed that this church was a bit different from the others where we had worked. Although small, the inside was constructed of marble and other quality materials. The nice leaders there actually happened to be an American couple sent from the Anglican church of Scotland to Honduras, Ecuador and finally, Bolivia. They cooked chili and other delicious American meals for us that I had not tasted in ages, minus the food poisoning!

My host family lived high above the city on Cochabamba Mountain, in full view of the Christ statue. They had three children in an English school and the father had attended high school in the States years before. My room was at the very top of their house in a loft, overlooking the entire city, which was one of the most amazing views I had ever seen. Our assignment now was to teach the youth of the church, which consisted of a few teenagers who loved to get drunk and use drugs, in evangelism and street ministry. I didn't know what doctrine they were being taught, but something was clearly not right. We set up a few evangelistic dramas in the central square but didn't have much response. That same night, we went out to eat with the youth, and they ended up asking me if I wanted to go to a club and if I knew how I would be reincarnated. I was befuddled at the confusing doctrine that seemed to be circulating.

The next night, we all gathered at the house of the American pastors for some youth ministry. The home was actually a million dollar mansion, complete with iron gates, over 20 rooms and quite a few missionary bungalows on the property behind it. It was the fanciest place I'd seen in all of Bolivia, even fancier than the cathedrals. After some focused prayer and ministry time with some of the worship leaders of the church, we turned to fun and games.

We were wrestling and bouncing around to reggaeton music, just having a grand old time. Around midnight, right in the middle of our roughhousing, the fun sent me head first into the hardwood floor, knocking me unconscious. I awoke in a pool of blood with faces staring down at me in disbelief as blood ran down my face and into my hands and then to the floor. I was quickly losing consciousness and passed out again. This time, I woke up in the emergency room of a Bolivian hospital after nearly 11 minutes of unconsciousness. The entire car ride with its bumps, bounces and turns did not even budge my limp 125 pound body. The doctors asked my name, my country of origin and why I was there. I couldn't remember much of anything at that point because I was in so much pain and shock. I was told that I had a concussion and that I had split my head open directly over my left eye. If it had been a fraction lower, I could have very well lost my eyesight in that eye.

They inserted a terrifyingly long needle into my face and begin to sew up the incision. Although they told me I wouldn't feel it, unfortunately, I felt every stitch even though I was unable to speak. I was admitted to the hospital overnight with severe migraines and an inability to sleep. Darin stayed with me for nearly 24 hours when the pastors came the next day to see how I was. I ended up missing our final celebration before leaving Bolivia due to my hospitalization and had to accept the horrible truth that I was about to face. In just a few days, I would begin a three-day bus ride back to Uruguay, without bathrooms or food and with this deep wound in my head. "Why me, God?" I wondered sincerely. After remembering our little experience entering Bolivia, I certainly wasn't enthusiastic about leaving, especially in this condition. The cherry on top of this entire situation was that we would be traveling on my birthday, August 6th.

The next day rolled around, and we said our goodbyes and thank yous to everyone from Cochabamba. I was told that the bus trip would be a little different this time as we would enter Argentina through a different border crossing. However, southwestern Bolivia has no actual roads through the dusty deserts. The bus would attempt to navigate the barren landscape despite this.

We conquered desert mountains, cliffs, cacti and dried up rivers. We also drove right through full rivers and past Oruro, where I took pictures and Potosi, where ancient rituals took place, including human sacrifice. We finally arrived at the Argentina border of Villazon. I honestly didn't think I would survive the ride. The heat was unbearable with no way to cool off, no water and nowhere to go to the bathroom. I had absolutely no space at all; in fact, I will venture to say that I had negative personal space. We walked with all of our things as my cart towered over everyone else's since it consisted of seven bags and one full box of imported American food that I intended to bring back to Uruguay. After piling all of our belongings on the road, we learned that our bus wouldn't arrive to take us over the border for another 12 hours. Nightfall came and brought freezing temperatures with it. We were all huddled outside under blankets, freezing our tails off. When the bus finally arrived, we were nearly frostbitten to death, and our group was scattered everywhere trying to recover all of our things. We were all so hungry and tired that we fell asleep as soon as our butts hit the seats. Of course, it wasn't long before we were awakened at Argentine immigrations, and I wasn't prepared for the events that followed. Time for another border crossing. Oh boy.

CRYING FOR ARGENTINA

After negotiating and paying additional fines, we arrived at Argentine immigrations, only to find that all of our bags had to be searched, including all seven of my suitcases and my box of extremely well-taped food! Everything had to come out, and then everything went back in. Little did I know that this would continue every hour or so all the way to the Argentine capital of Buenos Aires, almost a day's ride to the south of where we were.

Filing off the bus, tearing open all of my bags and my box of food and then rewrapping them all up until the next city was a nightmare. Apparently, a few kids with thousands of dollars' worth of cocaine made it through the border a few days before, so officials were really cracking down. We finally arrived in Buenos Aires the next day, then waited 12 hours for our bus to Uruguay. Being back in the capital of Argentina felt like returning to New York City from the Sahara desert – a great feeling! On my birthday, upon our arrival back at the YWAM base in Rivera, I didn't even receive a cake or anything. Everyone else who had birthdays while we were in Bolivia had been given a cake. The only thing I did on my birthday was go to a dirty, smoke-infested medical clinic to have the stitches taken out of my head even though they weren't fully healed - not a fun experience! The next day, to my surprise, my name was called, and I happily pranced forward to Darin's side to smile and receive my diploma. I couldn't believe it - I actually did it! Within a few hours, I had already bought my ticket back to Montevideo; I wasn't wasting any more time at that base. We had a graduation party and clean-up day, and I was the first one gone.

When I arrived at the bus station at Montevideo central, I was carting around a bicycle that I had bought at the YWAM base, my seven bags of luggage, and my floppy box of food that resembled a wet, ripped-up paper bag. Don't ask me how I managed, but somehow I did.

I called my pastor friend, who had kept in contact with me and helped me so much over the last few months. As soon as I stepped outside and stopped my baggage from falling all over the place, it started to pour down rain. By the time he arrived, I was soaked to the bone, and my luggage was also sopping wet. We went back to his house, managed to unload everything and plunked down on the couch, exhausted.

Over the next two weeks, we discussed my time at the school, how it had changed my life and what I planned to do next. The truth was, I had no idea what was next. I was quickly running out of money and buying all of my own food so that I wouldn't be a burden on the pastor and his family. I soon had to sell my bike and took frequent trips on my own to give the pastor and his family time alone.

Crying for Argentina

I traveled to other regions of Uruguay, seeing some beautiful sights and journaling.

I found myself crying my eyes out in a youth hostel bunk bed in Piriapolis, Uruguay. I knew that I was out of money and out of support. Even worse, I felt like God had left me and that the entire last six months of my life were a big dream. Now I was stuck, so I cried out in prayer over the next few days, and within that time, I received an e-mail from some fellow YWAM'ers inviting me to visit them in Chile. I had always wanted to visit Chile and had been praying for the opportunity.

The following Sunday, I announced to the pastor and his church that I would be on my way to Chile, and I thanked them for all of their support to me as a brother and a missionary. I said all of my goodbyes and dug through my luggage to get rid of whatever I couldn't use or didn't need. I loaded all of my things onto the bus for the few hours ride to the little city of Carmelo, to take a boat across the Rio de la Plata that divides Uruguay from Argentina. My friends agreed to pay for my trip, and I was off on another new adventure!

When I arrived at the loading dock, I jumped into a little seat on the little boat, headed towards a small subdivision of Buenos Aires, Argentina. Most of the time, I stayed outside on the deck, watching the Uruguayan shore slip softly into the distance. I didn't know when I would see Uruguayan soil again, but I was happy to be taking the next step in my journey.

Chili in Chile

(I didn't eat chili in Chile, I just thought it was a cool title.)

During the overnight trip from Buenos Aires, I woke up the next morning to notice a dramatic change in the terrain. The land was full of jagged mountains peaked with snow and magnificently carved valleys – in August! Within a few minutes, we pulled up to Chilean customs. After a long customs check and passport stamping session, we entered through the narrow jutting mountain canyons of Chile. I think my mouth was permanently open in amazement until we pulled into the Santiago Central Station. I had never witnessed such majestic beauty in my life, not even in the Swiss Alps! I immediately liked this place.

Upon arrival, my friend Marlene came to meet me. Once I arrived at her house, her family immediately invited me to stay indefinitely! Although I could see that a lot of the people had a significantly higher standard of living in Chile than they did in Uruguay, I knew that I couldn't stay too long. Over the next few weeks, I found that Chile was much more relaxed and less traditional, at least, from what I saw. The church that I was working with was full of dread-heads and young people with tattoos and piercings. I soon learned that the undergrounds of Chile are crawling with alternative youth culture, such as Goths and punks.

I was invited to work at a YWAM base nearby for a few days to help translate for a few American students who could not speak Spanish. Next, I was invited to Temuco in southern Chile. The traditional church in Temuco starkly contrasted with those in Santiago. I got some strange looks as I shared my story with the Sunday crowd. We had an opportunity to go high up into the Andes and minister to the natives, who live in little wood huts covered with snow and surrounded by wilderness. One small part of this amazing experience included the opportunity to drive around in my friend's truck at the base of three volcanoes – what a fantastic sight!

The food and hospitality were both wonderful, and I was really starting to love the country and wondered just how much longer my assignment would last. I became very good friends with an Austrian missionary and his family and after a great German-Chilean mixed dinner, I headed back to Santiago. I had been inquiring to see if I could use my accumulated airline miles for a return trip to New York. As it stood, I didn't even have enough for half of a flight back to the States. After praying for direction, a special offering came in from a pastor that I knew in Pennsylvania, and I was able to combine my miles with the money to take a flight to Texas and then on to New York!

My visit to Chile closed out my time in South America, but I wasn't just sure if I was ready to go "home." In fact, I didn't even know where home was anymore. I didn't know what it would be like to be back in the U.S. again after so long, and I was afraid to find out. However, I knew that it was time to go. A few days later, I said my emotional goodbyes at the airport in Santiago. I couldn't believe that I was returning to the U.S. After going through so much and spending a year in a different culture and immersed in learning the language! It would be a long flight back for me with time to reminisce on the last 12 months. Was this a dream or a reality? I was about to find out.

FINDING HOME

Upon my arrival to New York, my family did not even seem to recognize me as I walked toward them. Quite possibly, it had something to do with the fact that I was now 50 pounds lighter than when I left for South America. All of the walking and the Uruguayan diet certainly had an effect on me, but I honestly hadn't even noticed! When my mom and brothers recognized me, we hugged and hugged and then set off to get my baggage. I had gained quite an appetite on the flight, and I just had to have an American fast food fix on the drive home. I had not tasted that type of food in so long that I ordered two whole meals and gulped them down in record time! I repeated this feat a couple of times over the next few days, and I started to feel very sick. My body wasn't used to this kind of food anymore, so I began trying to eat healthily.

For the next few weeks, I just sat at home reminiscing about South America and preparing missions presentations for various churches and youth groups. I quickly realized that I would need to start bringing in funds as soon as possible since I was no longer on the mission field and my support had ceased. I spent a couple of days strolling around the small local townships of eastern Pennsylvania, applying for gas station jobs, which was the same thing I had been doing before I left.

Before I knew it, I slipped into a very deep depression. Life was very different in the States. I began to yearn for the strong community and relationships that I had built in South America. It seemed that no one had time to listen to my stories or understand much of where I was coming from at all; they were too busy. I had never heard of reentry culture shock, but I was plagued by it now. I started crying out to God about my condition asking Him to quickly intervene. It was even strange to speak English to everyone! I started to think that maybe I had served my time and that I should settle down, get married and have kids. Thus, I began to scan the church for eligible bachelorettes.

However, my own efforts were to no avail. One evening a few weeks, I was at our Monday night prayer meeting feeling more frustrated than ever. In fact, I stormed out of the meeting and into the crisp September weather to sulk in the parking lot. I felt hopeless and just wanted to give up. I had been outside pouting like a four-year-old for about 20 minutes when I saw someone walking to their car. I ducked down so that they would not notice me. I realized then that it was Millie, the crazy girl that I had met a year before. I didn't want to talk to her; I didn't want to talk to anyone. Actually, if I thought about it, deep down, I did want to talk to someone.

Just then, her car backed up right beside me, and Millie stuck her head out of the window. "Are you okay?" she asked intently. "Yeah, just a little upset," I responded. She seemed concerned about my well-being, and before long, I opened up to her. Over the next few minutes, I actually found myself enjoying our conversation. Although I wasn't interested in her romantically, I loved her hunger for the things of God and thought it would be nice to continue our discussion on the phone sometime. I decided to call her just a few days later. We had a nice, long talk about God and the Bible, and we seemed to have more in common than I had imagined.

As Millie and I began to converse regularly, she eventually invited me to come over to her place for a visit. I learned that she played the flute, which greatly interested me because I wanted to add a folksy touch to my one-man heavy-metal ministry project.

The following week, I decided to drop by and say hi. When I arrived, I was a little taken aback since Millie lived in a group home for the mentally ill. I wasn't sure what to think as I rang the doorbell. The door was opened by a very old woman with the shakes, and I waited patiently while she called Millie down. Millie popped her head around the corner at the top of the stairs and motioned for me to come up. I noticed everything in her room was spotless and in perfect little piles. I could also not help but notice that a random sleeping bag was lying in the middle of the floor. "A sleeping bag?" I wondered, "In her room? What is she doing, having a slumber party with herself?"

She was very excited about playing a song for me that she had written about the September 11th tragedy, and didn't waste any time whipping out her acoustic guitar and going for it. About 20 minutes later, while we were in deep conversation, I found out the purpose of the sleeping bag. She had not slept on a bed in a very long time; in fact, she only slept on the floor. She did not tell me why, and I did not ask.

Within a few weeks, we had shared a lot of personal information about our lives, and I found out that she was on many medications and had been to six mental hospitals by the time she was 19 years old. She had grown up with an abusive father and clearly believed many lies about herself. Her documented diagnoses included psychosis, anorexia, bulimia, suicidal tendencies, depression, bipolar disorder, post-traumatic stress disorder and borderline personality disorder, among others. This explained her rapid and frequent ups and downs. Many times, it was hard to be around her as I thought she could be quite unpredictable. I don't exactly remember when it happened, but at some point during that week or the next, I clearly heard the Lord speak to me.

"Rob, say hello to your wife."

Before long, Millie and I found ourselves sitting in a 24-hour restaurant at 4 a.m. talking about our relationship. I asked her what she was like off all of the medications, and she said that she did not know and that she was afraid to go there. She had been told that if she ever came off them, she would hurt herself - or worse. As I listened to her talk, I took notice of all of the long, deep scars running up and down her left wrist and arm from self-injury. They told a story in themselves and spoke volumes about what she had endured.

Regardless, I could not shake the feeling of destiny that I had pulsating through my spirit that night. I told her that I was willing to help her in any way that I could. I declared that Jesus could truly heal her for good and that she wouldn't need all of those medications to lean on. In that moment, we prayed together, and she made the decision to trust Jesus with everything, even her mental health. She opened up to me about several trips to the mental hospital over the years that included solitary confinement, the use of four-point restraints and various medications. Medical professionals told her that she would have to take the medications for the rest of her life. Despite this prognosis, she rose up in faith so quickly that she began to hand me her pills each day to flush down the toilet.

She had been like a lab rat for the doctors to test, and the anti-psychotic pills and mood stabilizers that she was taking did not allow her to feel or show emotion. Many days, we would pray together for hours, confessing and forgiving, renouncing suicide, self-injury and fear. She would cry and feel like she needed to be rushed to a mental hospital again. At times, she became numb and was convinced that I was going to call 911 on her, but during this time, I tried to show her that emotions are a normal part of life instead of an enemy.

We also began to address her eating disorders. The anorexia had a terrible effect on her body, and she looked starved and very underweight. She found it very difficult to accept food because she thought that she owed someone something for it or that the offer of food came with other stipulations. Growing up, she was severely punished for going into the refrigerator to get herself food. I remember one day when I had just started training as an assistant manager at a gas station. Millie popped in with her hair down and straightened, makeup on, with a piece of cheesecake. I had never liked cheesecake but that was the best cheesecake I had ever eaten! She always kept her hair up in a little ponytail, so her new hairstyle was a nice change. I spent my lunch break with her, and when she left, my heart ached for her.

One day, I surprised her with flowers and a little card at her job as a waitress. It was the best feeling in the world. Before long, the staff at her group home noticed the behavioral changes and wondered what was happening. Within a few weeks, they kicked her out because they found out that she was not taking her pills. When she was confronted, she announced, **"Jesus Christ healed me!"**

When she had nowhere to go, my mother cleared out a small spot in the basement and took her in. She even set up a little cot, which took up almost all of the space that was available in the small area. I can remember tucking Millie in for the first time just a few nights later. It was the first time that she was going to attempt not sleeping on the floor in a very long time. I told her that everything would be alright. On my way to work the next morning, I stopped by to see how she was. She had slept soundly all night! First, she came completely off her pills; next she slept all night on a cot!

Miracle after miracle began to happen. One night after getting doughnuts and coffee, I was seeing her off in the parking lot of the restaurant. Before she left in her little purple Hyundai that she called "Bullet," she leaned in close and looked me in the eyes.

Without any hesitation, she opened her mouth and popped out with "I think I love you!" She leaned over and quickly kissed me and ran to her car. I was shocked that she was so bold and that she was the one, not me, who had finally said those three little words!

I could barely reply, "I think I love you, too!" before she giddily hopped in her car and drove away.

Just a few months later, I began to think about proposing to Millie. A nice pastor came to my work every morning at about 6 a.m. to buy coffee for his church office, and we talked often about love and marriage. He really poured into me. After three months, I had decided to go ahead and put her rings on layaway. I secretly made payments every two weeks. She had no idea!

European Vacation. Sort of.

In December of 2006, I decided to take my last trip as a bachelor - to Europe. My plan was to travel and write, pray, think, and plan for the engagement and the future. When I took off on a flight to Frankfurt, Millie wouldn't let me go at the airport. It was very hard, but she finally left holding a globe and wearing my clothes.

When I arrived in Germany, I boarded a train with a Eurail ticket and traveled through the country to Austria, then back through Germany and north into Denmark. I saw so many beautiful sights, and although I had nowhere to sleep most of the time and I was freezing, I focused on writing in my journal.

Millie squeezing Rob at the airport – Dec. 2006

In Copenhagen, Denmark, I found a public phone booth to sleep in on a dark corner with drunken people all around me. I took a train to northern Denmark where I found a boat to Sweden. I roamed the streets of Helsingborg, Sweden for a few hours then returned to Denmark and headed southwest on the train into the Netherlands. In Amsterdam, I found some great architecture but quickly moved on to Belgium. In Brussels, I saw the Headquarters of the European Union and some other cool sights.

From there, I moved on to Luxembourg, which I loved! I wandered the frozen streets looking at the giant castles until about 3 a.m. when I found a hotel that gave me a tiny room the size of a closet to sleep in for 40 Euros. The room had a phone, and I called Millie at home in the States. She was ecstatic to hear from me, and we talked as long as we could without me going completely broke! I had found a beautiful letter that she had written to me, and I could not wait to talk to her again. From there, I traveled back to Germany and flew home to prepare to propose to her.

Just a few weeks later, we shared our first Christmas together! Up until this point, she had hated Christmas because of the horrible reminders of her past, but life was beginning to take on a whole different meaning for her now. I had thought about proposing to her on Christmas Eve or Day but felt that it was too predictable. I later found out that she was very disappointed because she thought I was going to ask her to marry me.

A week later, on New Year's Eve 2006, we headed to my family's house far into the mountains of Pennsylvania. On our way back, just as we were coming over the top of a mountain with lots of city lights below, I told her that I needed to stop and check the tires of the car. What she did not know was that I had hidden a giant candle in the trunk, which I was about to light and set on the side of the mountain. I loudly turned up the volume of our favorite song. I then left the car door open so that the music could be heard echoing through the mountains.

She heard me ask, "Millie, can you come here and help me?" The next thing she saw was me down on one knee next to a lit candle on the side of the mountain holding out a ring to her. "Will you marry me?" I proposed. She almost passed out and started to cry and laugh at the same time. I nearly had to catch her and carry her back to the car!

She agreed "YES," and I slipped the ring on her finger as we headed off to a New Year's Eve party to celebrate.

Tying the Knot

The helpful pastor who I had met at my job conducted our pre-marriage counseling and agreed to marry us on March 3, 2007. We decided that we would have a small, private wedding, but we wanted something different, of course. We decided on the theme of a Gothic-Renaissance style wedding and chose a spot outdoors by a beautiful lake with mountains in the distance. By the time March came, snow still covered the ground, and we scrambled around like crazy trying to get everything done in time.

The only place where we could find the themed wedding attire was at a Halloween store! We rented the outfits and made our final decisions. My best man, who dressed as a Viking, was a good friend of mine. Next was my brother Ryan, who donned a jester outfit. My little brother, Daniel, served as the ring bearer and dressed as a knight.

Millie had chosen her sister, Sarah, and a good friend of hers, as attendants. They both wore beautiful medieval gowns. Our unity candle was a large black castle, which was a bit difficult to light with the cold wind blowing! We had the flags of the world behind us, and I wore an archer outfit and carried a sword and shield. Millie looked beautiful as she came walking towards me, complete with bagpipes playing in the background. We then marched together to the make-shift altar, which was actually a red carpet on the lakeside, to an instrumental Christian heavy-metal song that we loved. I am sure that some of the guests were traumatized. Regardless of how they felt, this was the best moment of our lives. Tears welled up in my eyes as I pronounced, "I do" and kissed my beautiful bride.

When the ceremony was over, we headed to the reception hall at a fine Italian restaurant in East Stroudsburg, Pennsylvania. We enjoyed our first dance together as husband and wife. It was such a blessed time, and I just couldn't believe that even after the mess of the past, God had given me a beautiful girl who had been pure until marriage!

Rob and Millie's wedding – March 3, 2007

Following the reception, we took off to Canada in her

little Hyundai Elantra, which was now ours. We had written "Just married" in huge letters on the back windshield, and people would beep their horns in celebration. On the way to Canada, our ultimate destination for a freezing honeymoon, we stopped at a cozy bed and breakfast to spend the night, one of our wedding presents. The crackling flames in the fireplace kept us warm as we enjoyed the beautiful backdrop of snow out our window. That night, God began to pour out dreams and visions to us, and our marriage wasn't even 24 hours old!

The next day, we settled into a hotel in Ottawa, Canada with a beautiful view of the Canadian Parliament buildings. We enjoyed the Jacuzzi and fancy restaurant. Getting snowed in by a massive blizzard just added to our wonderful experience! We loved every minute. God had given us the grace to wait to consummate our relationship until marriage, and the experience of starting a new life together with our pasts erased was absolutely astounding.

On our way back to the U.S., we were stopped at the border because they found swords in our car. I told them that they were from our wedding, but they seriously doubted my story. I guess I could understand their reasoning. After a few hours of being detained and more questioning, they finally let us go home.

On our way home, I explained to Millie all about how God had called me and provided for me to go to the mission field while I was in Florida, so we decided that we needed to move there. The next day, we packed the car full of all of our possessions, including our cat and a street cat left to freeze outdoors, and we left for Florida. The only money we had was what was in our pockets from the wedding cards.

We had no idea of what we would do once we got there except we planned to return to the church that sent me on the mission field years before. We felt like God had showed us that we should move to Florida. We made one critical mistake - we did not seek Him on the timing.

Too Much Sunshine. Again.

When we arrived in Florida a few days later after an adventurous trip down Route 95, we searched for an apartment near where I grew up. This was a great opportunity because Millie got to meet my father for the first time. We found an apartment complex that had just been torn apart by a tornado, so no one wanted to live there. They were offering special move-in deals, and that was good enough for us! We signed the papers, unpacked our things and went to look for jobs. Millie found a job as a waitress, and I found a job as a cook and a second job as a manager–in–training at another restaurant. Millie worked almost 80 hours a week while I worked two jobs, and we began to rise up onto our own two feet in the world. We got another kitten and loved our little apartment.

The church had changed drastically since I had last been there, and it had grown so much that almost every time we went, someone would ask us if we were new. It was very frustrating, so I even tried to schedule an appointment to talk to the new pastor. The soonest available appointment was in two weeks, and when the time arrived, something else came up for him, so we never met. We quickly lost interest in church and ministry-related activities and stopped attending.

As time went on, we started to find ourselves falling

into a deep depression. We were both trying to be witnesses at our jobs, and some people expressed a little interest. However, we still felt that something was wrong, like a great void inside. We finally both got sick of working ourselves to death just to survive. Our air- conditioning bill was higher than I'd ever seen before, and you couldn't live without A/C in Florida! We were too tired to cook when we came home from work, so we would just order out every night.

We knew something needed to change, and one day while Millie was at work and it was my day off, visions of world missions and a spiritual awakening dropped in my spirit. I had not forgotten the call of God, but I had somehow put it on the back burner. I felt lost and tired, and I was ready for something different. We began to fall farther behind in our bills, and we finally sat down and prayed together. That same night, God made our next steps very evident. We felt like we needed to return to Pennsylvania. We thought about everything that we had worked so hard for and our new life together, and we decided that no matter how difficult, we would do it. Within a few weeks, we had given away most of our belongings, and were ready to drive all the way back to Pennsylvania. My brother Ryan had flown down to Florida to visit our dad and needed a ride back home, 1,200 miles away. We somehow fit him into our tiny overloaded car so that he could accompany us. We spent our birthdays on the road, thinking about our decision and what the future held for us back home. The truth is, we never could have imagined.

THE BEGINNING

It was so strange to be back in Pennsylvania. We had no idea what to do or where to go. Furthermore, my mom had just received a note from her landlord saying that no one else was allowed to stay at her place and that the house was under close watch. We were hoping to stay with her for a few weeks until we could figure out a plan. Everything certainly looked hopeless at the moment.

My first thought was that I wanted to find out what God was doing and where He was doing it. I didn't waste any time and called our friend Mark, an evangelist who had prophesied about our marriage and ministry nearly a year before.

"Yeah, brother, come on down to the Father's House in Easton! God's moving in revival here!" yelled Mark excitedly. He was happy that we were back and couldn't wait to connect with us. When we showed up to the church for a visit just a few days later, Mark was nowhere to be found. We were, however, introduced to Pastor Barry and his family. They were excited to meet us and so full of faith and passion to see God's church grow and flourish. They had moved from New Jersey to Pennsylvania some years earlier when they had felt God's heart for the broken, gang-ridden city of Easton.

The church was a medium-sized, rented building next to a pool hall, which made it a very strategic spot for evangelism. They had suffered much loss in both the leadership and the congregation but were passionate about rebuilding the church. We began to attend regularly and built thriving relationships with the pastor and his family.

During this time, we were sleeping on the floor of the neighbor who lived below my mother's apartment. We were showering at my mom's and eating anywhere we could. We spent the majority of our days seeking God for direction. We didn't have much money and had racked up some debt living in Florida. I knew that something had to happen and that it had to happen quickly.

We still felt strongly that God was calling us into ministry, so we began to put ourselves completely at His disposal. We began to help lead the evangelistic work at the church and took any available opportunities to talk to people about Jesus. Before long, we found ourselves leading people to Jesus in the streets, which then spread to local restaurants, businesses and so forth. Whenever we would ran out of money, a small offering would always come in from a completely unexpected source.

Just a few weeks later, we received an invitation from a relative to come and live with her. She owned a mobile home about an hour and a half away from where we were, and she was willing to provide us with a bedroom, our own bathroom and the kitchen. She worked from home and had some health problems and assured us that she would love the company. She offered the home to us as a form of support and asked only that we help her with upkeep and care of her seven pets. We were so blessed to have this opportunity, and we decided to take it. After a few days of cleaning and moving, we settled into the little mobile home in the mountains of Pennsylvania. Our relative's job meant that she had an available computer and Internet that we could freely use for ministry. We prayerfully designed a website to host our stories aimed at the "unlovables." We called our ministry "Messiah's Misfits." Our pastor gave me work with his construction company so that we could buy food and put gas in our car. The car, however, was old and was beginning to worry me. We weren't sure what steps to take next, but at some point during those few weeks, Millie and I found ourselves sharing our testimonies with Pastor Barry and Karen. We told them about our dreams and our vision to reach all of "Messiah's Misfits." Pastor Barry seemed to be very interested in what I shared and announced, "We would love to support that vision!" After all, he was young at heart and longed to see the lost come home. I was impressed to find out that he had actually played bass for John Lennon years ago in Madison Square Garden. We discussed the vision for ministry and various ideas a bit more.

Meanwhile, Millie and I started to apply for any jobs we could find, but "no" seemed to be the only answer we heard even though I was over-qualified for many of the jobs. I was frustrated.

The Beginning

Finally, a day came when we found ourselves completely lost, broke and overwhelmingly depressed. The trailer we lived in was far from civilization,and driving anywhere was expensive. We found ourselves using our last bit of gas to look for jobs when we pulled up to a Taco Bell and decided to eat with our few remaining dollars. After we finished and went back to the car, our evangelist friend, Mark, pulled up right next to us. He reported that the Lord had led him there, and he encouraged us for nearly two hours! Then he told us that he was having revival meetings in Quakertown and that we needed to come. He handed us some gas money, and without even thinking twice, we were on our way.

The revival meetings proved to be very refreshing, and the Lord moved powerfully! Over the next month, we went on to lead the worship and minister along with many other anointed people of God. We heard that there was a Christian festival happening nearby, and we thought it would be a valuable opportunity to network for ministry and meet new people. Unfortunately, though, most of the people attending seemed to be scared of us and didn't act like they wanted to get to know us.

At the festival, we met the regional director of a local Youth for Christ branch, and he seemed interested in our work. He decided to set up a date for an interview. Ironically, we were called for interviews to manage a nearby restaurant the same day and at the same time as the ministry interview. After time in prayer, we knew that in faith we needed to meet with the director of YFC instead of going to the other job interview.

The meeting went well, and we were accepted onto

142

YFC staff in no time at all. During the interview, we discovered that the positions were strictly volunteer, so we had to turn our faith level up a notch right then and there.

Almost every weekend, we would put out a "fleece" telling God that if He didn't act quickly that we would take it as sign to go and get jobs and forget about full-time ministry. This idea came from Judges 6 in the story of Gideon. God tells Gideon that he will save Israel through him. Gideon, however, wanted to make sure that he was hearing from God. Gideon put a sheep's fleece out and told God that if the fleece had dew on it in the morning, yet all of the ground was dry, then he would know God would fulfill His word. When he woke up and the fleece was wet with the dew and the ground was dry just like he'd asked, he told God that he wanted one more sign. This time, he flipped the request around – if the fleece was dry and the whole ground was wet with dew the next morning, he would know that God would act. God honored both of Gideon's requests.

I'm not saying that this is a formula that should be used in every situation, but we wanted to make sure that we were being led by God, and this is where we were at this point in our lives. As time went on, we began to learn to discern His voice more clearly, and we normally did not need to put out anymore fleeces. However, God did honor each of our requests and always came through for us, even when we wondered what He was doing.

In September 2007, we heard that a man named David Pierce was coming to speak in Connecticut, so we decided to drive out to see him. Someone had given me his book, "Rock Priest," years before, and he was a dynamic evangelist who we respected. We were very excited to finally meet him because his ministry had been a great inspiration to me for many years.

After six hours of traffic, we arrived at the church where he was speaking in Kensington, Connecticut. I couldn't believe it was really him. I had probably read his books more times than I had read all other books put together in my entire life.

He spoke simply yet very powerfully. After we listened to the amazing things God had done through his ministry in foreign lands, I knelt down and cried out to God for the nations. I stood up feeling so refreshed, and then I realized that David was standing right in front of us. "You drove all the way from Pennsylvania to see me?" he asked. They had announced that some people had come from that far at the beginning of the meeting.

We talked with David and told him how we would love to attend his school of radical evangelism in New Zealand. We asked him to pray with us that God would provide for us to come the following year. To our surprise he queried, "Why wait until next year?"

"Because we don't have the money to come this year," I responded.

He prayed with us, put his arms around us and declared, "As of right now, you both have full scholarships to come this year!" We were shocked, and Millie began to cry as I just stood there in disbelief.

At first I thought that maybe I had misunderstood

144

him. Apparently not! "Grab some applications and fill them out," instructed David. "I'll see you in New Zealand."

Faith Lessons

Needless to say, we had a very loud trip all the way home. We screamed and celebrated what God had done. He had just blown our minds again! Just a few days later, as we were headed to Easton on the Pennsylvania/New Jersey state line, I felt God telling us to go into New Jersey instead. The only problem was that the return toll to Pennsylvania cost 75 cents, which we did not have. I turned around, and we headed towards the New Jersey border. After we had crossed the free bridge going in, we stopped at a truck stop to ask God what to do next. We sat down on the pavement and started to pray. Within a few minutes, a friend that I had not seen in years pulled up, opened the door, and announced, "God told me you were going to be here!" She handed us 75 cents, and we headed back over the border to PA. It may sound far-fetched, but I believe God told us to cross the toll bridge just to test our faith.

That weekend, our pastor came to us and told us that he and the church wanted to begin to support us as missionaries. Within a few days, we received our first committed sponsors of $100 a month. It was clear that we needed to start sending out some type of updates, so we gathered together all of the emails of friends and family that we had, a total of 85. On October 5, 2007, we sent out our first newsletter. We had decided to focus on reaching the Pocono mountain region for Jesus, then the rest of the U.S. and then the world! We were a little discouraged to receive a few emails that requested removal from the email list and similar replies, but we also received some uplifting responses from people who believed in our calling. The Lord reminded me of a scripture in Zechariah 4:10 that encourages us to not be disappointed with small beginnings, and Zechariah 4:6 (NKJV): "Not by might, nor by power, but by my spirit, says the Lord of Hosts."

In that first week of ministry, we hit the streets of Easton and ministered to gang members and witches and even had opportunities to pray with them! We also worked with an evangelism team and saw 21 salvations in one day. On that same day, we had 24 bagels to feed the evangelism team, yet every person ate two or three. We quickly realized that God was in the miracle business on our behalf when He multiplied them! Below are some of our newsletter articles from the beginning of our ministry.

Newsletter #2: October 10, 2007

"On Sunday, we met a young boy, age 12, whose parents passed away a couple of years ago. His siblings are either in jail or in mental health facilities, and his grandmother, who has been taking care of him, is in the hospital. He was previously being watched by his aunt, who also recently died. He has been running the streets, doing drugs, drinking alcohol and wondering why he is here on this planet. Our hearts were absolutely melted for this child, whose name we will keep confidential. We were able to give him a drum lesson and spend a few hours ministering to Him, and for the grand finale, HE PRAYED THE SINNER'S PRAYER AND RECEIVED JESUS INTO HIS LIFE! Do you see how much the enemy of our souls has tried to steal, kill and destroy? Do you see how God wants to raise up a generation with purpose and restore their lives? We bound that foul spirit of death that his generation

146

held and then he told us: *"I'm afraid I will be left behind when Jesus comes back, I don't know if I'm saved."*
Now he knows - Praise Jesus!!"

Newsletter #3: October 16, 2007

"Just the other night we were sitting in a doughnut shop discipling a young man when we noticed that just across the way sat a young boy who had been alone for quite a long time. Since it was around midnight on a school night, we figured something was not right. After our session was over, we realized that he was sleeping, so we decided to go see if he needed to make a phone call, needed food, a ride or anything else. When we woke him up, we asked him if he was okay. We told him that he had been there a very long time and asked him how old he was. He told us that he was eleven. We weren't sure what he was doing out so late by himself, so we just prayerfully decided to talk to him. He was very hesitant to share and would not look us in the face at first. After about a half hour or so, we broke through a little bit. His name was Fawn. His mother had left him at birth, his father was in jail, and his brothers and friends were involved in street fighting and drugs. He lived with his aunt, who happens to be a witch, and his uncle, who is addicted to video games and hates church. When we started to share with him that Jesus loved him, he told us that he had never heard that before! We told him that Jesus died for him and has a wonderful plan for his life. We shared that there is a way to know that you are saved and that you aren't just born to die someday but born with a purpose. After explaining the gospel message and sharing our personal testimonies with him, he allowed us to pray for him. We then described how to receive salvation as a free gift, which he accepted! He said the sinner's prayer with us,

147

and together we welcomed him into the family! We are working to follow up with him now; please pray for him and his family!"

During the following week, I was in touch with a pastor who I had met on social media. He had a ministry that focused on reaching secular youth involved in the music scene, and I couldn't wait to work with him. I can remember the email popping into my inbox: "It would be great if you could come and give your testimonies in Decatur, Illinois, on Friday night, and then tour with us to different states and give your testimonies between bands!" To make things crazier, the tour featured a band from South Africa that was famous in the Goth scene. We could not believe it! We knew that God had opened a door, so we quickly responded and gave the pastor a big "YES!" Of course, the decision was completely in faith, and we only had a few days before we actually had to leave for Illinois. We had no money, our car needed to be inspected, and it needed to pass! We took it for three separate inspections, and each time, we were turned down. A few nights before we were supposed to leave, we were walking through a mall looking at all the nice things we couldn't buy, and I felt a tap on my shoulder. When I turned around, there stood a woman who we once met at a YFC outreach. "I feel like the Lord told me that you need money. Is there a ministry trip coming up that you are planning to go on?" she asked. We had not shared our needs with anyone, so we knew she must have heard from the Lord. She handed us a check and prayed for us! The next day, our car passed inspection, and we left the following morning for Illinois. We went from $0 to $500 in two days as everything came together in record time - another miracle!

Our First Ministry Trip

After 12 hours of driving, we stopped for the night in Indianapolis, to rest and reflect on what God had done for us while F-4 tornadoes danced around outside. We drifted off to sleep that night wondering what our first big ministry opportunity held for us.

Rob and Millie on their first ministry trip

149

The Beginning

When my wife and I arrived at the club, the scene took us by surprise. Even though the organizers were Christians, everything was designed to bring in the lost from the streets. We found a small back room downstairs so that we could pray and then headed upstairs to discern the atmosphere of the event. As we worked our way through the darkness, we saw many young people dressed in Gothic attire who looked like they were auditioning for a part in the Adams Family. The crowd was packed with gang members and occultists, and we saw extreme body modification everywhere. The longer that we stayed at the concert, the faster our hearts beat until we retreated back to the small prayer room that we had found downstairs. We were fortunate enough to find two other people who were hungry to see God move, so we prayed again and asked God to pour out His Spirit in the club. The air was thick, the resistance was strong, and fear consistently attempted to assault us in our minds. During a break between band sets, the time finally came for me to give my testimony, and we made our way upstairs. We strategically positioned our team throughout the crowd so that they could pray with anyone in the audience who was receptive. I hesitantly made my way to the stage to take the microphone. I had never given my testimony in front of such a rough crowd before, and my imagination ran wild thinking of the grim possibilities that might lie ahead. The place was completely packed out with many young people who had driven from other states to see the featured band that was playing that night. The dark atmosphere added to my feeling of intimidation and just seemed to encourage those who glared at me... with Halloween makeup plastered all over their faces, of course.

I grabbed the microphone and stepped off the stage

so that I was directly in front of the crowd. Silence fell throughout the club as I stood there trying to muster up the courage to say something. After introducing myself, I quickly dove into the details of my childhood and my journey into witchcraft and satan worship. Within just a few moments, some in the audience seemed to be drawn into what I was saying. As I spoke, a tall man with a harsh look on his face inched closer and closer to me. His face was painted with evil clown makeup, and he wore a hat with the symbol of a world-renowned gang. I glanced to the side of the stage to make sure Millie was okay, and I continued. "God is not a liar! Jesus revealed Himself to me!" I cried, as I related the details of how I had a powerful, life-changing encounter with Jesus Christ. "He delivered me from sin and bondage and gave me a new life, and He can do the same for you tonight! I know there is someone here who can identify with what I'm saying, and I want to talk to you tonight." I then challenged the crowd to pray and ask Jesus to reveal Himself to them. I also dared them to allow us to pray with them. Although the details are hazy, I can remember that I felt weak and shaky - until the name of Jesus came out of my mouth. Suddenly, a great boldness fell on me, and I was able to finish speaking. I quickly moved in with Millie and our team to talk with people individually.

Within a few moments, my assistant whispered in my ear. "Rob, someone wants to see you outside… *alone*."

"Oh boy," I thought. Sure enough, the man with the evil clown makeup who had been glaring at me menacingly wanted some privacy with me. I turned toward him, and he motioned in a most sinister fashion for me to follow him. As I trailed him down the stairs and out the door, all I could think was, "Lord, if it is my time, I guess I'll be seeing You any minute now." I then remembered seeing this same man in the middle of a switchblade fight with another gang member when we first arrived at the club. Uncertain about where we were going, I reluctantly followed him behind the building into a dark alley. He finally stopped and faced a brick wall. His back was turned to me, so I could not see his face. As I waited in suspense wondering what came next, he slowly turned, and revealed his tear-stained face with makeup smeared down his neck.

Between sobs, he managed to choke out, "How can I be saved; how can I know Jesus?!?" My thoughts quickly jumped from thinking I was going to get shot in a dark alley way to helping him respond to the Gospel right then and there!

"Kneel with me now!" I said in amazement.

He dropped to the ground, took his hat off his head and threw it into the road. In tears, he relayed that he had recently been released from a mental hospital for murdering his younger brother. Through his brokenness, he explained that years ago, he had a dream when voices spoke to him and told him to obey them by carrying out this evil deed. He confessed to all sorts of things that would make your flesh cringe, but in that moment, I knew that he needed to know the forgiveness of Jesus. I had been in this same situation - desperate to know that I could be forgiven. He was crying out from the pain and agony tormenting his heart. I looked him in the eyes, and I declared, "You are forgiven of these things because Jesus died for your sins and rose again, overcoming sin and death!" Without hesitating, he prayed with me and confessed Jesus as Lord.

As he prayed, he began to scream, "Fire! Fire! I feel fire in my chest!" He clutched at his chest as he fell to the ground. For a second, I wondered if I had prayed the wrong thing or if he was dying. Then Holy Spirit spoke to me and told me that He was bringing a fiery baptism to this young man from the inside out.

"This is the Holy Spirit!" I explained, "And you are a whole new person!" Suddenly, as we knelt there on the sidewalk, a car pulled up in front of us. Before I realized what was happening, the doors opened and out jumped two large men proudly sporting their loyalty to the opposing gang of my new-found friend. They began circling us as we knelt on the sidewalk in the dark.

"They're here to kill me!" the young man exclaimed.

"Well, at least we're going to heaven!" I exclaimed. We closed our eyes, prayed harder and braced for the worst. Suddenly, everything went quiet. We peeked out. No men. No car. No danger.

"We're alive!" the young man announced, lifting his face from the ground. I couldn't believe it! The men had just disappeared moments after threatening our lives. As we walked back toward the staircase, my new friend suddenly fell to the sidewalk, gripping his chest and rolling on the ground!

"What's going on!?" I shouted in disbelief.

"FIRE!" he shouted. "FIRE!" "My chest is on FIRE!" Peace washed over me as I understood that Holy Spirit was filling the him with holy fire. "It was like fire in my chest that spread throughout my whole body!" he proclaimed as he rose from the sidewalk with tears in his eyes. I took him back inside where I hurriedly located a Bible to give him, and he hugged me and tearfully thanked me for sharing that night.

A MISFIT REVIVAL

The next day, we continued on to a suburb of Chicago, Illinois, where I was able to preach my testimony again in a club. It seemed that atheists were the only ones who attended this show. Here are some of the original newsletter articles from this trip:

The next day, after about four hours of sleep, we headed to Chicago where we ministered in a much bigger venue. The same bands were performing, and we talked to the head of the venue to open up the little store they had in the building so that we could pray in a different environment away from the loud music. We went in there and started to pray when the leaders charged in with a drunken 16-year-old girl who ended up on our laps in a panic, screaming about how all the Christians in the world are liars and asking how we know for sure that God is real. It was hard to communicate with her because she wasn't coherent. She was not willing to let us to touch her while praying for her, so we prayed from a distance because she started to get violent, flailing her arms around and screaming. We prayed

155

that God would sober her up, and she eventually threw up, just in time for Rob to go up and give his testimony to the seemingly more vocal crowd than the previous group.

When Rob went up on the stage, he spoke powerfully, yet certain people started loudly mocking him. Others covered their ears and rushed for the doors when he mentioned that we were missionaries. He ended the same way he did the night before by asking them to come to one of us to pray if they were curious. During his talk, the girl who had previously been drunk came up and thanked and hugged me. I gave her our email, set her up with some leaders for help and told her to keep in touch. When Rob walked off the stage, the next band got up and started to perform.

A lot of kids came up to us that night wanting to know more, but one in particular caught our attention. He came up to Rob and swore," What the **** man? I mean, what the ****?" Rob looked at him and replied, "Excuse me?" As a small group was gathering around to hear what was going on, we discovered that this boy was a hardcore philosophical atheist who was none other than the main person scoffing at Rob during his speaking. The boy apologized for mocking and later approached us to know more about Jesus. By the end of the night, he reluctantly agreed to let Rob pray for him and described a strange presence during the prayer that felt good. His final remark was "Thank you, man, tonight you just might have changed my life." Rob replied, "Just remember, it wasn't me but God working through me as a vessel to reveal Himself to you." People are following up with him, and he is attending a church in the Chicago area. – Millie

Many other people heard the gospel message and came to Christ that night. Here is another account that has just been e-mailed to us:

"Hey, Rob, my name is Greg, and I was at the show last night in Berwyn, and I heard you tell your story. I was the guy who gave you a hug right after you got off stage. I gotta say man... God bless you for having the strength and the courage to go around telling people your story. I can't even imagine how hard it must have been going through all the things you have been through. You changed my life from your speech; you opened my eyes. After I gave you a hug and thanked you, I had to go walk around the block because I was just so overcome with emotion. You are my hero, Rob."

Of course, we wrote him back and let him know that Jesus is his true hero, After all, Jesus died for him; Rob didn't. This is just another example of a life touched by the Spirit of God.

The next night in Grand Rapids, Michigan, proved to be an awesome night of ministry to the bands with whom we were working. The main band, which happened to be from South Africa, was very touched by Millie's testimony as she preached alongside Rob. They explained to us that they wanted to go deeper, but they were not accepted in South Africa, especially by the Christians and the racial groups. They had gone through similar things as Millie in their lives, and they were very impressed by our boldness with the Name of Jesus. It was a very emotional night, and even though the last band blatantly mocked us as they ultimately mocked Jesus, God showed Himself very powerful, and we made many connections for future *ministry. In addition to many salvations, by the end of the tour, EVERY band except the mocking one was talking about Jesus from the stage in front of everyone! That shows you the power of speaking the name of Jesus boldly; it's contagious!*

After we arrived home, a young man from Chicago somehow got a hold of our phone number and called to threaten us. He insisted that his main calling in life is to "silence the messenger." However, for some reason, he couldn't go through with it and instead, told us that he wanted to listen to what we had to say. He made it very clear that he hates Christians but then claimed to be involved with an infamous gang and wanted to know how to get out. We talked for a few hours, and he is very much considering giving his life to Jesus. He said that he would like to stay in touch through e-mail. Please pray for him!"

It wasn't long before churches began to hear the stories of what God was doing in these clubs and in the lives of the young people, and they started inviting us to come and share. As the end of the year drew near, we found our schedule completely full of bookings for ministry events, churches and evangelistic tours. We spent the following months touring Pennsylvania and Maryland, seeing God move miraculously and providing for us every step! Through the majority of these travels, we did not have a dollar to put in our gas tank, but God always made a way. This newsletter sums up a few of our activities during that time:

Newsletter #5: 11/07/2007

We've had another action packed week here, focusing on Pennsylvania. As God continually pours out His grace and love for the lost, we've witnessed salvations, miracles and divine provision!

Here are our latest updates:

• With barely any time home from the Midwest, on October 24, we ministered to the Father's House youth group in Easton, PA. We told them of all the wonderful things that God did on our previous ministry trip, and one young man got filled with the Holy Spirit. We also got to pray the sinner's prayer with another young man that night; He is receiving follow up as we speak!

• On October 26, we headed south to Waynesboro, Pennsylvania, for a rock concert outreach to the street kids. We traveled with a Christian Goth band and shared our testimonies while they set up their equipment! The leaders were very thankful to have us come and reach the kids on their level. Many were touched, and we will be returning to disciple the Goths and new believers there.

"Dear Rob and Millie,
I wanted to thank you so much for sharing your testimonies at Waynesboro, PA. I was there and it really touched me and gave me hope for my sister who is in some serious need of Jesus Christ. God bless you in this mission!"
– Anonymous

• Upon our arrival home Sunday morning, we gave some testimonies of the awesome things that God did on the

previous ministry trip to encourage the body of Christ. Millie prayed with a young girl to receive salvation - another soul for the kingdom!!

• On October 30, we shared our testimonies at Legacy Ministries in Easton, PA. When we were done speaking, we opened up the time for questions and prayer as lines of kids waited to speak with us. Millie spoke with a few girls who had heard of Jesus before but were victims of rape. She prayed with them and directed them to local professionals for counseling and discipleship. Some others were partially involved with witchcraft and wanted to be free.

• On Halloween, we traveled to Quakertown, PA, to encourage believers there about how God is moving and changing lives.

HIGHLIGHT

"Sometimes I hit my mother and beat my cats because of all the hatred I have inside," explained the young boy. "My mom's boyfriend is a cocaine addict, and they both hate me. Everyone calls me a child molester, and I get beat up in the alleys almost every night." I wasn't sure how to react to these statements. We were at Legacy Ministries in Easton, PA, ministering to a crowd of unsaved kids. This young boy was crying out for help, and my heart broke for him. "I want to be cool like you", he commented. After a good half hour of talking, he showed me scars all over his arms and told me that there was someone there who wanted to beat him up. I began to pray for him and his family, and he told me that he had no knowledge of God or the Bible. I told him that Jesus is the only person that could change his life. I explained the gospel in a simple way, and right there, we prayed, and he asked Jesus to come into his heart and life! He then told me that he had to walk home alone across town, and the last time he did this, he was beaten up and left for dead. We arranged for the pastor to bring him home, and he thanked us with a great big hug, one of the first in his life. He is now being discipled through Legacy Ministries.

Newsletter #6: 11/26/2007

On the 24 of November, we traveled to Binghamton, New York, for a Gothic outreach event. As usual, we knew that if even just one person was touched, then the whole trip was completely worth it, and after some heavy prayer, we proceeded. As we were giving our testimonies, we noticed a young girl sitting all the way in the back. She wore black lipstick on her lips and dark makeup on her eyes. I felt very strongly that the Lord wanted to touch her that night. At the end of the event, I was upset to find out that she had already left. I asked about her and found out that her family is a mix of alcoholics and atheists. I was told that she had been around before but had a lot of issues with rebellion. As we were packing up our equipment to leave, a man came through the side door of the church and stopped in front of me. He seemed a bit lost, so I asked him if I could help him. He said "Yes!" He reeked very strongly of alcohol, and I wasn't sure what to think. Just then, he mentioned, "I just wanted to say thank you." Somewhat stunned, I replied, "For what?" "My daughter has been at the house ranting and raving about the message that she heard tonight. Something really got to her. Something really touched her." He spoke sincerely.

161

A Misfit Revival

Upon realizing that this was the same young girl's father, I smiled and asked him to hold on while I ran to get something before he headed to the door to leave. I returned quickly with a copy of our testimonies on CD and our ministry card. "Give this to her to listen to from us. I think it will encourage her and maybe even your whole family can listen to it!" "Thank you," he replied, "I will!" With that, he left. Just when you think that who you are or what you're doing is insignificant is when God shows you that He uses the most simple, ordinary people to accomplish His purposes. They are being followed up as we speak. Please keep them in your prayers.

This outreach was featured in the newspaper in Binghamton. It read as follows:

"Goth group scheduled to perform at church. Experimental Goth group will bring their music and drama to the catacombs at 8 p.m., Saturday at Community Baptist Church, 743 Chenango St., Port Dickinson. The reverend of the church has said that the group includes a married couple who calls their ministry "Messiah's Misfits" and speaks to those attracted to the darker side of the music and arts world. A donation of $5 is requested for admission; use the church street doors to enter the basement level."

Things were really opening up! Just as our schedule began to fill with events as far away as New York and Ohio, our little purple Hyundai's engine suddenly failed. I remember thinking, "We cannot cancel our engagements; God will provide a way for us to go!" The following newsletter article tells more of the story:

We were definitely caught off guard by this

circumstance, and without a vehicle, we felt totally helpless and unable to continue in our missionary work. We took some time to seek the Lord on the issue, and we were not surprised when He told us to keep all plans as scheduled. We had no idea how we would make it to New York or Ohio per our itinerary, but we knew that we just had to walk by faith – completely! After driving our pastor's work vehicle around for a little while, a friend of ours approached us and shared that he felt that he should let us borrow his car for the next two weekends in a row. We praised God for this opportunity as we did not have to cancel our prior engagements! Although this did not take care of our vehicle problem, we decided not to lose hope or grow discouraged. At the same time, we felt led to sow an extra offering, and God told us to sow a cruise to the Bahamas that we had won back in April to a family member. Within ONE DAY, we received a phone call from a different loved one, who said that it was on their hearts to give us a CAR! They told us that they would not only give it to us but make the monthly payments on it until it was paid off! What missionary support! We are so encouraged, and the Lord has provided a manual 2003 Dodge Neon sports car for us to continue the work of the Lord! Be encouraged, and be obedient to the Lord! You won't regret following Him! Also, last week at one of our outreach events, we had the opportunity to minister deliverance to a couple with alcoholism and the occult plaguing their family and marriage. They renounced these things, among others, and together, we proclaimed deliverance and healing! They are very involved in a good church and outreach program. Please keep them in your prayers.

The testimonies did not stop there but increased! We worked hard for the harvest through Christmas and into

January and saw amazing results!

On November 26, we headed to a secular underground nightclub and bar in New York City. The crowd consisted mostly of married businessmen who had just gotten off work to come and meet ladies at the bar, late night partiers, and local Manhattan kids roaming the streets. The plan was to present our drama, which depicts our testimony and redemption by Christ at the cross. Upon our arrival, we immediately did not feel so welcomed. We started to unpack our things and introduced ourselves to some of the people there, the other bands and bartenders, etc. We met a man who was performing without his other band members because he was from Amsterdam, and they couldn't all make it to the U.S. for their tour, so he decided to go alone. He started to explain to us about how they got their band name and the background of it all. He went into the fact that the name of their band was some satanic religious practice in which they had this crazy party with drinking, drugs and ritual sacrifice. When asked about where he comes from, he described Amsterdam as a place of complete freedom because of the options people have to do things that you can't openly do here in America. We were able to befriend him, and he ended up thinking that our reason for being there was really cool. We were able to leave there with an open door into his life as we made an impact for Jesus. Over time, we talked to many different people, one of whom was the bartender who came up to us and asked, "Are you all underage or do you just not drink?" She couldn't figure out why the whole band wasn't accepting free drinks like the other bands did. We had a great open door to speak to her about why we were there. She was really receptive to hearing about it. As we talked, she eventually told us that she was born in New Zealand!

At the end of the night, she came to us with a huge smile, asking us if we had any more dramas because the one we did was so powerful, and she really felt something. We felt led to give her our testimonies on CD and our contact information. It was a very powerful night, and we are believing for the harvest from the seeds that we planted in NYC. Here is Millie in the club holding a cross.

We returned home very early the next day with just one day left to put together and plan for the big outreach concert event being held in Easton. That night, we planned

events and brought in the band as about 30 kids showed up. After the band played for a while, we had an intermission to hold a hackey sack contest, present our drama and give our testimonies. It was so powerful and the kids were so attentive that when we were speaking, you could hear a pin drop - quite unusual for this age group! By the end of Rob's testimony, he announced, "If you are curious about this Jesus, and you want to know more, or if you're ready to make a serious commitment to Jesus tonight, please follow my wife into the back room. Prayer counselors will be available to help answer your questions and give you more information on what this really means. Approximately 15 people responded! We had 10 first-time salvations and about five recommitments. We are still in the process of following up on them.

By December 1, we were already on our way to Sandusky, Ohio, to once again present our evangelistic drama. The atmosphere in some of these bars can be far from welcoming. Many times we are not permitted to say much, but in submission to the leaders there and setting a positive example of Christ's humility, we go and do as much as we can and let God make the impact He wants to make without obnoxiously pushing or shoving a message at people and making them feel uncomfortable. We strive to set the best example of Christ's love without shame or hiding our purpose for being there, but at the same time respecting the wishes of the leaders who invite us. Sometimes this goal is not the easiest one to attain, yet we went and when we showed up, to our surprise, the night held a different type of flow. It was a metal/thrash/hardcore night. We received some pretty nasty looks, and when it came time to do the drama, everyone just stared. When the music stopped, it was silent for a couple of seconds. And *then you could hear a voice chant, "More! More!" from the crowd as cheers and claps, hooting and hollering, soon followed. This was not what we had expected, but we weren't opposed to it! Later that night, many people came up to us to ask questions and tell us how cool they thought it was. One man in particular, who was bald and a pretty tough-looking guy, came up and enthused, "Hey, that was awesome! I really enjoyed the shooting up and popping pills thing. What was that all about?" Right then, Rob took him aside and was able to give him our testimonies and explain all that Jesus had done for us. At that moment, the guy hugged Rob and said "Man, that rocks. That's really great." Rob gave him one of our CDs and took his contact information. It was a strong night of seed planting!*

Unfortunately, bad weather over the past week has led to the rescheduling or cancellation of a few of our events. Please keep us in your prayers. On a positive note, we were able to update the websites and follow up on the salvations and recommitments.

Highlight

The night of the Easton outreach, after many of the kids had left, a girl was crying in the prayer room. I decided to go up to her and ask her how she was feeling, what was going on and invite her to talk if she needed. She shared with me how hurt she was. Her father died of a drug overdose back in 2001, and one of her mom's boyfriends had died of the same thing in their house. The night he died, they went to bed with the dead body in the house until the next day. She never got to talk to anyone and never knew where to turn. She once tried to tell her mother how she felt, but her mother bought her a pack of cigarettes and advised her, "This will make you feel better." I watched this girl shaking as she was speaking to me with tears literally streaming down her face. She went on to tell me that she didn't know what to do anymore, and she ended up idolizing a singer as she worshipped him, prayed to him and meditated on his music. I asked her if that ever helped her in any way and she admitted that it did not. She kept telling me that she feels as if she's screaming in a room full of people with no one listening, and no one to hear her. All she wants to do is talk about what she is going through, and she just wants someone to hear her. I was able to tell her more about my testimony and ask her if she'd be willing to give her life to Jesus that night because He DOES hear her, and she answered, "Yes!" Right there, she said the sinner's prayer, and I hugged her. It was a powerful night, and I am also believing for her emotional healing from all that has happened. I'm arranging for professional help to be provided for her as well. Please keep her in your prayers. These are the very reasons why we are doing this. Each of these situations breaks my heart and the heart of the Father as well. I remember being in similar circumstances, but this would all be in vain if I didn't know that I know that there is hope. And now, she has hope. More hope than she's ever had before. I ask that you please keep her in your prayers along with the millions that her story represents. -Millie

Christmas Newsletter 2007:

On December 11 and 12, we had the opportunity to minister the gospel to a large group of unbelieving Gothic and rocker kids in Waynesboro, PA. We had a great response, and many of them requested a copy of our testimonies on CD. After our message, we took a group of them into a back room to pray and answer questions about Jesus and religion. We had a great time building friendships and sharing our faith with these young people, and we are looking forward to visiting with them again next month! We are currently discipling them online and answering questions; please pray for them!

On December 18, we headed back to Legacy Ministries to deliver a powerful word given to us by the Holy Spirit. Many young people were touched as we explained how Christ's blood paid for their sins and how they were bought with a price. We talked about forgiveness, callings and destinies; many of the youth from off the street are really beginning to know the Bible!

SEISMIC REVIVAL
AND THE SOUTH PACIFIC

Just a few nights before Christmas, Millie and I were soaking in the Lord's presence in our room in our little trailer when we had a powerful experience with the Lord. We had recently attended an event in Harrisburg where we saw Todd Bentley, an evangelist from Canada who really inspired me, David Herzog, another minister from Arizona, and a few other speakers. We had been challenged from that point to go even deeper in God. It was around 3:00 or 4:00 a.m., which was when we saw the Lord's manifested presence the strongest in that season. The glory of God fell in the room. Millie did not usually fall and get drunk in the Holy Spirit at this point, and she was pinned to the ground for hours by the power of God! She eventually had to go to the bathroom, and she pulled herself along the ground, half-crawling in an attempt to make it to the toilet. I was not in a much better position myself and could barely help her! As I knelt in a fetal position, I glanced up behind me and saw a white figure standing over me with long white hair and eyes that were flaming like fire. I shrieked in terror and awe and hid my face in the pillow beneath me. His presence was so strong; I quivered and actually felt like my spirit was going to leave my body. The Holy Spirit announced to me,

"Rob, I am going to bring forth a revival of seismic proportions. It will shake the earth like it has never been shaken before, something that history books will not even be able to record."

I was consumed with His presence and the vision of this "seismic revival." I began to see mass crusades and salvations in the Spirit. Whole cities and nations being shaken and healed, coming to Jesus! From that night, Millie and I both began to walk in a new anointing, and we knew that we had touched just the hem of the garment of the manifested glory of God.

Needless to say, this was a wonderful way to start off 2008! God had already planned for us to start out the New Year ministering in New England – and in the same exact spots that I lived and played with Stratia years earlier. Actually, Millie and I ministered in the same venue in Connecticut where my band had our first show in 2003! The powerful events throughout New England yielded much fruit. Overall, God used our time in New England to provide the money for us to buy the plane tickets to New Zealand for February! Before we left, we saw God's power poured out in many places. Here are some accounts from our newsletters of our ministry:

Massachusetts

After a five hour drive on January 4, we prepared

to challenge a large crowd of mainly young people to live radically for Jesus through our evangelistic drama and the sharing of our testimonies. The response was great as many teenagers came to talk to us and thank us, as well as parents who were there to cry out for hope for their children who were lost. We were able to pray for these prodigals as well as give them some ministry resources to sow into their friends' and children's lives for salvation! The pastor was so touched that he invited us to come back the following Sunday where we were able to share more in depth about our ministry and vision. Thank you, Massachusetts team!

Connecticut

The next day, we made our way to Ashford, Connecticut, for another concert outreach. Over 100 kids packed the small concert hall, and after performing our drama and speaking for over an hour, the presence of the Holy Spirit filled the place! We were able to minister to and pray with many kids who were dealing with a variety of issues such as drug addiction, eating disorders, suicide, etc. One young man told Rob that he was addicted to cocaine, and had hung himself two weeks before in a failed suicide attempt. He wanted to be saved and free of his addictions. After Rob prayed for him, he cried uncontrollably and grabbed a brand new pack of cigarettes from his pocket and ripped them up in shreds! Many hearts were touched in Connecticut, and follow up is taking place. The doors to return to Connecticut in the future remain open.

Maryland

The Lord touched many in Hagerstown, Maryland,

172

where Rob was able to speak to a large group of homeless men with various problems and addictions at the Hagerstown Rescue Mission. After praying with the men for first-time salvations and boldness for the already saved, we were able to freely distribute testimony CDs to every man there! Many were very encouraged, and one even shared that he is just coming out of a major gang lifestyle and wants to live for Jesus!

Pennsylvania

Waynesboro, PA -

On January 16, we returned to Waynesboro, Pennsylvania, for continued outreach to the Gothic community. After a message and some testimonies, eight of the Gothic kids knelt together with us to respond to the gospel. Others asked questions and told us of drug addictions and lifestyles that they are fighting to give up. Two decided to be baptized! We praise God for this victory, and they are being followed up as we speak. We also had the opportunity to give a seminar on sub-cultural evangelism to bring a better understanding of modern youth culture and their need for Jesus and unconditional love. The Holy Spirit touched many and deposited a fiery passion for the lost, no matter how different or "extreme!"

Bushkill, PA -

On January 20, we presented the gospel to a young crowd of mostly high school students through our drama and message, explaining sin and redemption through the blood of Christ. We then gave a call for those who did not want the world's lies any longer and wanted to live radically for Jesus to come up front and kneel with us. Eight young people came forward and publicly confessed Jesus, including some with issues of self-injury and depression. They are currently being followed up by godly mentors!

As we spent more time in the secret place with the Holy Spirit, we would see more power and anointing flow out of us and our ministry. We began to seek God for deliverances and healings as well as salvations. Here are some accounts from February:

Pennsylvania

"I have Legions, and they could kill you right here and now," threatened the young man, staring into my eyes with large, black, gaping pupils. "If I don't accept God now, they will make me kill myself." Millie and I looked at each other and asked, "Are you ready to do that?" "Yes," replied the young man, starting to cry and shake. We explained that he MUST desire them to leave and allow the Holy Spirit to guard his heart, or they could come back worse. He agreed, and we began to pray over him and commanded the demons to come out. He was thrown into an emotional frenzy, then he calmly confessed Jesus as Lord and Savior with us in tears. His eyes changed and now looked normal, and he hugged me for a while before leaving. This young man, along with many others, received deliverance and renewed strength through repentance and prayer recently in Easton, PA. On January 29, thirteen young people from the streets of Easton publicly responded to repentance and rededication to Jesus. On January 30, the youth of Easton repented before the Lord and cried out for revival. On February 6, we continued our Youth Revival

Service with a teaching on "how to discern God's voice." Many of these young people are being raised up mightily in the Lord's army as we speak!

Illinois

"Satan!" screamed some people in the crowd as we performed our evangelistic drama and began to preach our testimonies from the stage. "If you feel a tug on your heart because you want to give your life to Jesus tonight, ignore your mocking friends and come up here and kneel with us!" Amazingly, we watched 20 kids make their way forward at a secular death-metal concert. They all prayed to receive Jesus with us out loud, including some in the audience as well. We then had them fill out follow-up cards. Afterwards, the lead guitarist of one of the death-metal bands took us back stage to tell us that he felt something and wanted to know Jesus. He prayed with us right there to receive Jesus, and the presence of God came down in the club! We then conducted two ministry training and follow-up services on Saturday and Sunday with many in attendance, including a witch. God moved powerfully to equip the Christians for ministry and to nudge the hearts of the unbelievers in that place.

Maryland

After a weekend of ministry training and teaching on callings, evangelism and missions, 30 young people came and knelt with us to take a stand to live radically for Jesus, no matter what the cost! Some kids literally were shaken and touched by the presence of God! Somebody told me that it was the first time there had ever been a response like this in this certain conservative church group. Please pray for God's continued guidance and call upon these young people's lives!

Before we knew it, the end of February had arrived, and it was time for us to board the plane for the South Pacific. The time had just flown by, and it was also almost our first wedding anniversary! We had a stopover in the Fiji Islands for one night, so we decided to take advantage of it and celebrate our anniversary there. On February 27, we flew to LAX and prepared for our overnight flight to Fiji. As we were walking to our departure gate, I was glancing at restaurants for somewhere to eat when I saw a familiar figure. The back of his head was buzzed, and his neck was full of tattoos. I instantly thought to myself, "Is that Todd Bentley?" I grabbed Millie and moved up to get a closer look. Sure enough, it was him! I couldn't believe it! I had seen him on God TV and at a conference a few months before and was very touched by his testimony of deliverance from drugs and darkness. I approached him and asked, "Excuse me, are you Todd Bentley?"

"Yes, are you with us?" he questioned in response.

"WHOA, we could be!" I thought! I told him of how his ministry inspired me and that we, too, were evangelists, and he asked where we were going. "New Zealand," I answered. "Us, too!" He replied. "We have a conference/crusade in Auckland in a few days!" I couldn't believe it!

Before I could think of a reply, one of his assistants handed me a card, and Todd responded, "When you get to Auckland, go to the town hall and show them this card. We would like you to minister at the crusade with us!" I thought I was dreaming, and then he prayed for us. As we walked away, I was astounded by God's amazing networking power! Many times in our ministry, God has connected us with others in places that I would least expect. I quickly emailed our pastors to tell them what happened. While on the plane, we met a nice missionary couple who were taking Bibles to Fiji. Needless to say, this family thought that I needed to get saved, and I was afraid to talk to them. When we finally did talk, it again was a divine connection from God, and they are deeply involved with our ministry to this day.

When we arrived in Fiji, we were greeted at the airport by big men in skirts with guitars singing, "Bula, Bula, Bula!" Bula means "welcome" in Fijian. The driving was on the left side of the road, which was quite a shock for us, and we soon found out that it was rainy season on the island. There were mud slides everywhere, but we did manage to find a taxi that would bring us to a cheap place where they rented cabins, except the taxi driver charged quite a bit extra because he had to maneuver through a lot of mud. We found an inexpensive beachside bungalow with a hay roof and settled in. The beach was dirty and washed out, and the bungalow had a mosquito net over the bed. This was the first time that we would have to sleep with one of these contraptions! Millie plugged in her hair straightener with our international plug kit only for it to explode within a minute. The heat was horrible, and our stay in Fiji was already full of mishaps. We tried to make the best of it, but because we are really not tropical beach-loving people, it proved a bit difficult.

We hailed a taxi into town and got a bite to eat. We had to stay clear away from the road because people would nearly run us over, and we didn't know which side of the road to walk on because of the confusion with driving on the left-hand side of the road. Everywhere we went, we were hounded by the nuisance of people begging and wanting to sell us things. Just then, a large man came out of a little souvenir place and called us in. I thought it may be an opportunity to witness to him, and we reluctantly agreed. He sat us down and began to tell us the history of cannibalism in Fiji. We were quite uncomfortable, but we listened anyhow.

The man continued, "We on Fiji time now," He then handed me a big clay bowl, which looked like it was filled with dirt water. "Drink," he commanded.

Millie shot me a look, and I knew what it meant. DON'T DO IT! I responded, "No thanks."

The man then growled, "You a missionary, and you need to respect our culture, no? This is our culture." With that, I sucked it down. It was extremely bitter and instantly made my throat numb. He then insisted that I down the entire contents of the bowl.

We had come into town to find Millie a bathing suit, and here I was, gulping down this nasty dirt water. Finally, we decided that it was time to leave. I was feeling very weird, and as we got up, another man came over and put necklaces on me. When I tried to take them off, he motioned, "No, they are a gift from us."

Millie and I shrugged and turned to walk out when the first man started yelling "Hey! You can't steal my necklaces! You must pay for those!"

Now I was angry and sternly declared, "STOP IT, NOW" and took the necklaces off and quickly walked out. When we arrived back at our bungalow, we heard that the one behind ours had been broken into, and all of the guests' passports and money had been stolen. "Okay," I wondered, "Lord, can we rest at all today?" Thankfully, our bungalow had not been burglarized. We decided to put on our bathing suits and just try to relax in the pool. We had barely gotten any sleep, and the heat was making us even more tired. As soon as I got into the pool, I realized that my whole body was completely numb, and I could not feel if I was moving my legs or not! They had drugged me. We prayed and rebuked the drugs out of my system, and within about an hour, all of my feeling came back. Needless to say, after barely sleeping again in a mosquito-infested oven in our bungalow, we were happy to return to the airport for our flight to New Zealand.

New Zealand was one of the most beautiful sights I had ever seen! As soon as we arrived, we made our way to Auckland town hall and showed them the card that Todd had given us. They refused our entry, but then someone from the ministry came out and told them we were with them! We were given seats up front near the stage with the ministry team badges to wear. Within a half an hour, we were called up to begin to minister to people! The situation was definitely more radical than I had ever seen or experienced. I just began to pray with people, and they would fall over, some crying, some screaming. I was amazed at the supernatural activity and knew that it had nothing to do with me. After both meetings ended, we went backstage and spent time with Todd to get to know him better. I had no idea what God was preparing us to enter once our time in New Zealand ended.

Seismic Revival and the South Pacific

Getting settled in beautiful New Zealand for five months was an incredible opportunity. The culture was very different from that in the U.S. although we speak the same language. We nestled into the little retirement town of Waikanae, just north of Wellington.

Classes started, we took subjects such as Hermeneutics, Worldviews and Evangelism, Worship, Creative Outreach and more. Within no time, we began to plan outreaches in the community. The youth of New Zealand deal with a very high rate of suicide and gang involvement with gangs such as the Mighty Mongrel Mob and Satan's Slaves, just to name a few. We looked forward to seeing heaven invade New Zealand.

We enjoyed meeting the other students at the school, who had come from the U.S., Poland, Germany, New Zealand, Australia, Switzerland and Brazil. The fun antics of the Brazilians made me feel right at home. I translated from English to Portuguese for them, which reminded me of my days in South America. We worked with great people on ministry strategies. We had wonderful times there, and one of the girls we grew the closest to, Abby, was from Colorado. She loved heavy metal but was a worshipper at the same time. Millie and I had so much in common with her. Here are some of the reports from the ministry events where we worked together:

Our first outreach was in a skate park in Waikanae, New Zealand. We gathered our talents and came up with unicycle riders and fire-breathing and also handed out water and hot drinks in disposable cups with Bible verses written on them. Near the end of the outreach, Rob stood up in the middle of the skate park on top of a ramp with the fire breathers lighting him up to attract attention and gave his testimony. He explained salvation, and then yelled *"DO YOU WANT TO KNOW JESUS?"* We heard the voice of a young skater boy respond, *"YEAH! I DO!"* Rob continued, *"IF YOU WANT TO KNOW JESUS, COME UP HERE AND ACCEPT HIM INTO YOUR LIFE RIGHT NOW!"* and 10 skater kids came forward to give their lives to Jesus that night! Eight of the 10 showed up to the follow-up Bible Study we had the next Tuesday and have been coming since!

Paraparaumu Outreach:

We held another recent outreach in a skate park in a nearby town called Paraparaumu, New Zealand. (Don't try and pronounce it!) We had similar attractions at this event, including fire -breathing, drumming, flags, tea, cookies and a marionette show that depicted the truth of Jesus. At the end of the marionette show, the leader gave an altar call and some of the kids came up to pray and recommit or receive Jesus, and many were touched. We stayed for a while longer to talk with the groups of drunken kids in the park, and they shared many things with us. They told us that three of their friends had already committed suicide that year. One of them was a very rich drug trafficker, but he couldn't find satisfaction, happiness or any purpose in his life, so he ended it. It was a great time to build relationships with these beaten-down youth and pray for them. We will continue to reach out to these young people one prayer at a time. This is a generation in need of a Savior. They want and are searching for purpose and a reason to live. They strive for happiness and approval. Jesus wants to give them more than they can imagine!!!

During our short time in New Zealand, we learned of four suicides, the youngest, a seven-year-old. Some of the students started to complain of nightmares and weird things happening. We knew that the enemy did not want us there, but we realized then that we must've been making a difference! Abby told us just a few days later that she had woken up and seen a little girl at the end of her bed. When she sat up to look closer, the little girl's head shrunk down to the size of a tiny head, and the eyes popped out of her face! All of the students prayed over her together, and the encounters stopped. We needed to come against the spirit of suicide and death, which we were about to encounter in even a stronger way.

Face to Faceless

One night around 9:30 p.m. near the middle of the school, Millie and I were walking to the house of some fellow students. We usually took a short-cut through the neighborhood, which led us to the next block nearly in front of their residence. This night, however, was different. No one was home when we arrived at the house, so we turned back. When we took a right out of the driveway, we saw someone in the distance. They were still far away, having just emerged from the beach a few blocks down. The entrance to the beach was visible from where we were; the only thing partially blocking our view was the trees. This person came from that spot. We didn't think much about it when we first saw them because they were so far away. We continued to make our way down the street towards the entrance to the short-cut. As we walked, the person approached us and began to come into focus.

After a minute, Millie and I stopped and looked at

each other. Something wasn't right. The only lighting shone from one street light, which meant the area was fairly dim, but I could still see the figure approaching. As it grew closer, both of us could see that the head of the figure did not match up with the strides of the body, arms and legs. It seemed as if the different body parts were floating! It stopped about 20 feet in front of us.

By now, we could clearly see how unusually tall the figure was. Its complexion was powder white, and it had black clothes on. Instantly, I suspected that the subject in front of me was not human. Before I could say or do anything else, Millie motioned me towards the path we originally planned to take. As it stopped in front of us it turned around. I approached it from behind to take a closer look. It then levitated about two feet off the ground as if it were being hung at the neck by an invisible noose. We could not believe our eyes, and when I realized that the creature had no face with hair moving around in spirals as if it were alive, we turned around and RAN.

We took off down the short-cut path through the houses, praying all the while. We didn't know what kind of unearthly creature we had just seen, but we didn't want to stay around to find out! As we were running, we turned around to see if we were being chased. To our horror, the creature was hovering over the ground and coming after us as if it were traveling at the speed of light. It moved very quickly without even touching the ground! It did not seem limited by time or space and moved in intervals of time. For example, every three seconds or so, it would move another 100 feet instantaneously.

We ran all the way to our friends' house, who also

happened to be the leaders of the school. They were not home, but we found their door open. We barged in and frantically slammed the door. When they came home about a half an hour later, they found us hiding in their kitchen. After explaining to them what had happened, we went looking for the creature, but it was nowhere to be found! When we returned to our small house where we lived with other students, we weren't sure how to tell them or if we should even say anything at all. However, we asked if we could join together and pray because some weird things were happening, and they agreed. Before we even shared, another good friend of ours told us that she wanted to say something.

"The other night, I was out prayer walking on the beach around midnight. There was not much light, but when I turned around, I saw a white figure come out of the water. It was tall with long lanky white legs. When I saw it, it did not look human, and I started to run back to the house. It chased me all the way to the road, and then it disappeared!"

I got the chills and flashed Millie a surprised look. Our friend had described the same figure that we had just seen. With that, we decided to begin praying.

As soon as we started praying, our friend Melly from Germany came tearing out of her room screaming, "THE DEVIL IS IN MY ROOM!!! HELP!!!" After we calmed her down, she told us that satan appeared over her bed and was laughing at her. She decided to pray with us, and then we determined that we should anoint the spot where we saw the demon and pray against the spirit of suicide and death. We believed there was only one reason that we saw it get hung. It occurred to us that we should not have run when we first saw it but rebuked it on the spot! We headed back in a friend's car, stopped at the spot and began to pray. We did discern the spirit of death, so we rebuked it.

It was clear to us that we weren't welcome in the sleepy little New Zealand town, which became more evident as our time there drew to a close. One of our good friends was threatened with a knife by a local Maori man when attempting to display a cross on Easter. As we prepared to leave the city, we began to receive invitations to minister in other parts of New Zealand. We found a responsible couple and turned over the Bible study to them. They promised that they would continue getting together with those who had received Jesus the night that we preached at the skate park. Just before we left, the house of one of the young men that was coming to the Bible study burned down - and it happened to be on the same street where we had seen the demon just a few weeks earlier. As we traveled the North Island of New Zealand, we again saw God do amazing things everywhere we went, including many salvations and healings. Just before we were scheduled to leave to come back to the United States, I was talking with our pastor in Pennsylvania and he mentioned, "Rob, have you heard what's happening in Florida with Todd Bentley?"

"No!" I answered, "Todd Bentley is in Florida?" "Yes!" he replied, "A mighty revival has broken out. The sick are being healed and the dead are being raised! It's being broadcast live on God TV every night! It's no coincidence that you met him!"

I couldn't believe what I was hearing. During my time in New Zealand, my vision for mass revival had increased, and I couldn't wait to get back to the U.S. to contact Todd. While we were in New Zealand, my good friend Aaron had called us to tell us about a dream that he had. In the dream, he saw Millie and me preaching before thousands, and they were being saved, healed and delivered. He told me that he believed that if we continued on faithfully, these things were going to come to pass. As I heard about what was happening in Florida, I recalled that dream. What could God possibly be planning now? The last thing that I did before leaving New Zealand was to again ask God for the nations. Prayer is powerful.

Rob and Millie in New Zealand

THE FLORIDA OUTPOURING

Upon our arrival home from New Zealand, the first thing we did was pray about the next step. Our first Sunday back in our home church, this phrase popped into my spirit: "Rob, you will go to Florida." I couldn't believe it. We'd only been home about four days, and we had no money at all. "How are we going to go to Florida?" I wondered, "How will I convince Millie to go?" Our last Florida experience was not so good. I decided to tell our pastor what I felt the Lord speaking to me. He instantly agreed, and thus, the idea was confirmed.

I informed Millie about what I felt that the Lord had said, and I watched as she shrunk back in disbelief and gulped loudly. "Well, God's going to have to tell me, too!" she snapped.

I responded, "Okay, if it's Him, then He will." The next day, she felt strongly that Florida was, in fact, what the Lord was saying, and we began to pack our car for the trip. I still had no idea what money we would use to get there, but I had learned that when God tells us to go, He will provide. I found a card that Todd Bentley had given me in New Zealand months before and decided to call them to ask if they needed any help with the revival.

Sure enough, they answered, "Get down here!" The day that I called, one of my friends was over and desperately wanted to go and experience the revival. I then received a phone call from another friend that I had not talked to in a long time but who was also looking for a ride to Florida. She was deaf in one ear and believed that God would heal her there. When they told me they would take care of the gas money and fly back home, it struck me that God had provided in record time yet again! Early the next morning, we left for Lakeland, Florida.

After driving about 20 hours, we checked into a hotel and went straight to the revival tent. The air was alive with an electricity that I had never felt before. The presence of God was so incredibly tangible, and it was instantly addicting! I watched as person after person was immediately healed by the Holy Spirit and as thousands received Jesus. The woman with the deaf ear that had come with us from Pennsylvania was healed instantly that night! We all went back to the hotel room amazed at what God had done.

Our friends were only staying for one more day, and then Millie and I would be on our own. I didn't know where we would sleep or how we would eat. The only thing I could think of was how consumed I was by the spirit of revival that God had sent to us. The next night, I went to the ministry team to tell them that we had arrived from Pennsylvania to help in any way that we could; however I was not ready for what they said next.

"Okay, follow me; you're going to be working on the stage tonight."

"WHAT?" I thought, "The stage?" There were around 13,000 people there that night with a live broadcast from GOD TV to hundreds of nations. My job was going to be catching those who were touched by the Spirit of God and to help maintain order on the stage. At times, the anointing became so thick on the stage that I could not even stand, let alone help someone else stand!

After our friends said goodbye, we waited in expectation and excitement to see how God would provide for us to stay there and serve. The next night came, and I found myself on the stage again in front of all the cameras, not believing that I was really there. Millie and I knew that we had nowhere to sleep that night, but we carried on in faith. Around 11:00 p.m., a man from South Africa approached us and announced, "The Lord told me to give you this." He stuffed cash in my hand and turned around and walked away. I ran to Millie and told her what the Lord did. We knew that He was going to provide, and it was so exciting to see the manifestation of His miraculous provision! Little did we know, in the not-so-distant future, that we would be in similar situations much farther from home. The $200 that the man gave us allowed us to rent a drug- and bug-infested motel room for a week but also gave us some great ministry opportunities.

The next thing for God to supply would be food. Each night, it seemed that someone invited us out to dinner or lunch the next day. We also went to a church food pantry that supplied us with snacks to sustain us throughout the day. Before we knew it, the first week had passed, our time in the hotel was up, and we had not gone hungry once. Millie and I both felt that we were going to be in Florida for a while, so we began to look for a more permanent place to stay even though we did not have a steady income. Millie was training to work backstage with those who were being healed and recording their testimonies, and I had moved into a security position on the stage. Every couple of days, someone would come up to us and tell us that God told them to give us money. No matter what need we had, God always provided it. We ended up renting a small apartment, living on offerings as people that we never met before gave to us.

This bug-infested apartment was in the middle of a neighborhood with many drug dealers; however, a short trip to our local Walmart made it cozy, and it seemed like home. We ended up having a wonderful time ministering to some of the local people who lived in the apartments close by, including one who became a believer and was baptized live on God TV! She even came to feed the poor with us and minister in the streets.

After a few more weeks, Millie and I were both offered full-time paid positions working for the Florida Outpouring. We were able to rent our own mobile home and buy a new baby kitten that we named Abigail, after our dear Colorado friend that we had met in New Zealand. Working at the revival gave us full access to the action almost 24 hours a day!

Before long, Millie and I moved to working in the live call center of the Florida Outpouring. Our job was to pray with people calling in from all over the world and minister to them over the phone. We saw many results in the first few weeks as we served in this position and encountered some of the most miraculous testimonies over the phone in Lakeland.

Almost every person that called in with an urgent prayer request called back within a few days with an amazing testimony of how the request was answered! I remember one man in particular whose father had just suffered a heart attack, and he was being rushed to the hospital to undergo lifesaving measures. Less than an hour later, the man called back and said that his father was in open-heart surgery right then, and the doctors were confounded because every artery in the man's body was completely blocked, yet his heart had started beating again! Testimony after testimony came in, and our faith grew and grew. We longed for God to use us to do crazy things like these!

The leaders of the revival regularly organized anointing lines. The revival was drawing to a close, and the last such prayer line was scheduled. I ran in at the very end of the night and was last in line. Before I knew what was happening, Todd pressed the anointing rag onto my head twice and screamed, "DOUBLE PORTION!" He then handed me the rag. As I walked away from the tent feeling the heavy presence of the Holy Spirit, I stopped and looked down at what I held in my hand. It dawned on me that I was holding a symbol of the anointing of the Holy Spirit – and I believed in impartations! I ran to Millie, told her what had happened and anointed her with it. We were so excited that God had given us the same anointing rag that was used to anoint thousands of people for a transference of the Holy

Ghost!

Less than a week later, Millie and I were on the road again at the direction of the Holy Ghost. We once again gave away our possessions so that we could travel throughout the U.S. and release what we had received. We were continuing to move forward in complete faith, and God provided yet again. As we left Florida in our car with not even enough money to make it to the next state, we stopped at a thrift store to say goodbye to some friends that we had met there a few weeks earlier. When we arrived, they commented, "The Lord told us to give this to you guys." We were shocked! They handed us an envelope, which enabled us to travel through 26 states over the next few months. We drove across the country, connecting with many of the contacts that we had met in Lakeland and watching God do amazing things in each place!

When we reached South Dakota, we attended a festival in the city of Sioux Falls where most of our friends from New Zealand would be for an evangelistic concert. Upon seeing everyone, we shared stories of what we had been doing over the last few months and where God was leading each one of us for the future. During the festival, we stayed with our friend, Abby, and her sisters, who had flown in from Colorado, as well as a few other friends who were with us in New Zealand. After volunteering to serve at the festival together, we headed to Minneapolis, Minnesota, to spend a few more days with them and visit some local ministry bases.

During this time, a friend called us from Florida to inform us that our kitten had died. We had given her to him to watch over until we returned, and he had accidentally stepped on her. She was so badly injured that she did not make it. Although this may sound childish, Abigail, our kitten, had brought us joy through some difficult times while working for the revival in Lakeland. We forgave him, knowing that it was an accident, and the following night, we took our friend Abby out for dinner. We were happy to spend time with her as we shared what had happened and told her that we were so glad to have her, our Abigail, in our lives.

She told us that night that she would love to come to Pennsylvania to visit and possibly do a Gothic outreach with us! We were excited because it seemed that people were starting to catch our vision. After saying our farewells in Minneapolis, we headed towards Madison, Wisconsin, to minister at an event called "Nights of Fire" and then drove on to Illinois once again. We could not even believe the increased anointing that had taken place in our lives! Deaf ears were opening, addictions were instantly broken, and people were running to the altars at our meetings!

Upon our arrival back home in Pennsylvania, we were already strategizing for local revival ministry and evangelism opportunity. We decided to withdraw from the public eye for a few months to seek the Lord for the next step and enjoy family time. During that season, Millie and I created a website and organized an email list again simply dedicated to our personal teaching and preaching ministry. We were excited to launch into a new year.

As 2009 started, we felt led to fill a need in our church concerning discipleship. God then put the desire in our hearts to run a 12-week intensive discipleship school. We had about 25 students quickly sign up, so we ran with it!

As we taught on themes, such as world missions, spiritual warfare and preaching and teaching, we started to feel that familiar missions bug creep to the surface. We prayed about what God wanted us to do with the remainder of the year after the school was done.

Another Sad Goodbye

Just a few weeks after we held our discipleship school graduation, we received the call. The phone dropped from our hands as we sunk down in disbelief, and our eyes began to fill with tears. The words echoed though my head,

"Abby died in a car accident last night in Colorado."

Our dear friend Abigail, who we had worked with in New Zealand and recently spent time with in Minneapolis, had gone to be with Jesus. I was scheduled to preach at our home church the following morning, and it was one of the most difficult things that I ever had to do. We sent flowers to Abby's family in Colorado and took a few weeks off to mourn our dear friend. In Abby's memory, we vowed that the day the Lord gave us a baby girl, we would name her Abigail. We were now more determined than ever to bring hope to the nations, and not one day went by that I did not think of the legacies of my friend Mike – or Abby.

**In memory of Abigail Cortese –
October 10, 1987 – January 24, 2009**

GOSPEL TRAFFICKING

Both Millie and I had Latin America on our hearts for some time, and the call began to ring more deeply within our spirits as the days turned into months. Although Millie had never been to Uruguay, she also felt a strong call to the nation that I so dearly loved. We prayerfully decided that we would venture to Uruguay together in the coming months to release what we had received in our recent ministry experience. We created vision points and organized fundraising for our next mission. We had learned that "where God guides, He provides."

However, a few weeks after publicizing our vision, we crunched the numbers and knew that we needed to wait and pray. One night, I retreated to my prayer closet. "Just tell me what you want us to do already! I'm tired of guessing!" I cried out to God. At that moment, came the familiar voice of the Holy Spirit.

"Rob, I want you and Millie to be *My traffickers*."

"Your *WHAT*?" I wondered.

I heard it again. "My traffickers."

"Okay," I thought, "I must not be hearing God."

Then came the voice again. *"I want you to traffic My presence and My gospel to a dark, lost world."* Now that made a little more sense to me, so I sought more information. Over the past few days, Millie and I had been watching the news about the terrible violence happening in Mexico with the drug trafficking wars, so the term 'trafficking' was familiar to me.

It was right at that moment that a vision exploded into my spirit – so strong that I was flat on the ground. I saw a map of the Americas roll out before me, and a red line drawn from the southern United States through Mexico and all the way to Uruguay. I knew in my spirit that this was the route that we were to take. "WHAT? ARE YOU SERIOUS?" I cried out to God. I felt the Lord tell me that a trail needed to be blazed for the gospel **by land** from the U.S. to the bottom of South America. "Lord, don't You know how dangerous that would be?" I asked.

Somehow, in my spirit, I actually saw us going through with this crazy idea. I ran out of the closet, white as a ghost! Millie watched me in confusion as I ran across the room and plopped down in front of her. "God wants us to be His traffickers," I announced.

She stared at me blankly, waiting for more details. I ran over to the giant world map on the wall and traced the line through two continents that God had shown me. "This is our route," I explained. She looked at me in disbelief with her mouth gaping open.

"Well, God's going to have to reveal it to me, too!" she admitted. That was actually okay with me because I did not like the idea of taking my wife into the middle of such chaos!

A few days later, Millie came to me and asked, "So, when do we leave?" I couldn't believe it! God had revealed the same thing to her, and we both had received confirmations in our spirits about the trip. We quickly started studying the situations in each country that we would pass through. That night, as we were researching Mexico, we were so grieved by what we read that we could not even continue. The swine flu had broken out, and the drug wars were growing so bloody that innocent tourists and civilians were victims of kidnapping and murder. We decided to take one last look at a major government-based travel website, which warned us not to travel to Mexico for ANY reason. We knew it was serious. We prayed a bit and came to the conclusion that we should skip Mexico.

However, a few days later, we received further confirmation in prayer that we were **not** to skip Mexico, but we felt that we were to blaze a trail for the gospel through **all 21 nations** of Central and South America. We arranged a meeting at our pastor's house shortly thereafter and presented them with the vision. They were quite impressed and also felt that it was, in fact, God. We were thrilled to have their full support. Together, we decided that on May 16, 2009, we would walk across the border from Texas to Mexico with no return date. Our mission would be simply this: Traffic the gospel. We concluded in prayer that we would complete the journey once we had the opportunity to minister to the lost in each of the 21 nations. However, we prayerfully set the condition that we were only allowed to travel by land and sea as necessary, and air travel was off limits until we had completed the journey. This was to be the ultimate "Holy Ghost Amazing Race!"

Over the next two months, we spent much time in agony in our prayer closet. The more we researched each country, the more we did not want to go there. When we started studying Colombia, we both felt nauseous and asked God once again to confirm that we were to traverse through the nation by land. Colombia had the highest kidnapping rate on this side of the planet due to the FARC, or Revolutionary Armed Forces of Colombia, aka terrorist guerillas. I had seen numerous documentaries of many, including Christians, who had barely escaped from them with their lives.

I honestly don't think I've ever gone through anything in my life like what I went through during that season. I could better identify with Jesus' struggle in the Garden as He agonized, "Not My will, but Yours be done!" I was ready to trust God like never before. I printed out a map of each country and put them together in a small book to take with us on our travels. In order, the countries we would be covering were: Mexico, Belize, Guatemala, El Salvador, Honduras, Nicaragua, Costa Rica, Panama, Colombia, Venezuela, Guyana, Suriname, French Guiana, Ecuador, Peru, Bolivia, Argentina, Chile, Paraguay, Brazil and Uruguay.

We had no idea how long the trip would take, and each of us would tote a camping backpack as our living quarters. We didn't know if the money that we had raised would even get us through Mexico. We did not know how we would make it to South America from Central America without taking a plane. All that we knew was that we were asked to go. As we spent our final moments with our family, friends and pastors, we didn't know if anyone would ever see us again. We had no malaria pills, no way to get home from the jungles once we arrived, and no contacts in most of the countries that we planned to visit. It was very hard to say goodbye to everyone that we loved, but we had the drive in our spirit to get out there and start trafficking the gospel, no matter what the cost.

After spending a week in California with some friends before we left, we flew to Texas and prepared for the grand departure. As we approached the Mexico border, we thanked God that no matter what the outcome, He would receive all the glory. We observed everyone who marched to and fro with masks on their faces to protect them from the swine flu. We had made up our minds, and there was no turning back now. Peace flooded our hearts as we crossed into Mexico, and the only thing that we desired was this:

So likewise, whoever of you does not forsake all that he has cannot be My disciple. Luke 14:33 (NKJV)

Whether in Asia, Africa, Europe, South America, North America, Australia – or hey – even Antarctica, for that matter, we want to be faithful to the call of Jesus. It may require us to forsake our own dreams, our own goals, even our very life. Wherever it may lead us, no matter what the cost, we want to be ready and willing to say, **"Here am I, send me."**

200

Revs. Rob and Millie Radosti have traveled to nearly 30 countries together and are the founders of Rob Radosti Ministries. They are best known for their encouraging shows, intensive mini-schools, conferences and extensive pioneer mission journeys, especially to the Native Americans of Alaska and Canada. Their vision is to help you discover your origin and destiny in Jesus Christ. To invite them to your city, please visit **RobRadosti.com**. Rob and Millie love to receive your prayer requests and testimonies!

Be sure to follow Rob's official Facebook page at

Facebook.com/RobRadosti.

Please consider financially partnering with Rob Radosti Ministries for the Kingdom! Thank you for your generosity.

Also, remember to visit the RRM online store at RobRadosti.com for exciting resources!

Made in the USA
San Bernardino, CA
29 May 2016